High Profits from Rare Coin Investment

New Revised Edition

Q. David Bowers

Published by

Bowers and Ruddy Galleries, Inc. / Los Angeles, California 90028

International Standard Book Number (ISBN): 0-914490-03-6
Library of Congress Card Catalogue Number: 74-76717

_____

First Printing: April 1974
Second Printing: April 1974
Third Printing (with price revisions): November 1974
Fourth Printing (with text and price revisions): November 1977

_____

Also by Q. David Bowers:

Coins and Collectors
United States Half Cents 1793-1857
Early American Car Advertisements
Guidebook of Automatic Musical Instruments, Vol. I*
Guidebook of Automatic Musical Instruments, Vol. II*
How to be a Successful Coin Dealer
Encyclopedia of Automatic Musical Instruments*
How to Start a Coin Collection
Value Guide of Automatic Musical Instruments
Collecting Rare Coins for Profit

(*Designated as "one of the most
valuable reference books" by the
American Library Association)

Note: The past performance of coins as an investment is not necessarily an indication of the future, for it is important to remember that the future is always unknown.

Appreciation is expressed to Kenneth Bressett of the Whitman Publishing Company for permission to use certain information from A Guide Book of U.S. Coins. Appreciation is expressed also to Mrs. Marion Russell, editor of Coin World, in which Q. David Bowers' weekly "Numismatic Depth Study" column appears.

The following Bowers and Ruddy Galleries staff members helped in the ways indicated: Robert Budinger and Phil Starr, photography; Lorraine Gillman, Nancy Kane, and Glinda Vallow, composition, proofreading, and layout; Judy Cahn, John Murbach, James F. Ruddy, Nancy Ruddy, and Karl Stephens, Jr., research; Beryl Williams, compilation of statistics.

Contents

ABOUT THE AUTHOR . . . Q. David Bowers is a director of Bowers and Ruddy Galleries, Inc. of Los Angeles, California, one of the world's largest rare coin firms and a subsidiary of General Mills. He is a member of the International Association of Professional Numismatists, the American Numismatic Association (Life Member 336), the Royal Numismatic Society, the American Numismatic Society, the Numismatic Literary Guild, and other organizations. He is a director of the Professional Numismatists Guild and is a recipient of that organization's coveted Founders Award. His weekly column, "Numismatic Depth Study," has appeared in "Coin World" for many years and has earned him several awards. In addition he has written for all other major American numismatic publications—as well as many outside of the rare coin field (the "Encyclopedia Americana" and "Readers Digest," for example).

With his business associate James F. Ruddy, Dave Bowers has been an advocate of rare coins as an investment for many years—long before coin investment was a popular subject. His great experience in the field forms the basis for the present book.

Dave's other activities include a deep interest in antique music boxes, orchestrions, and related items. His 1008-page book on the subject, *The Encyclopedia of Automatic Musical Instruments,* is a classic in its field and has been designated by the American Library Association as "one of the most valuable reference books." He is a director of American International Galleries of Irvine, California and Copenhagen, Denmark—a leading firm in the antique field.

Although Dave travels frequently, Southern California is his home. It offers "an ideal combination of coin activity and a pleasant climate," he says.

Chapter 1

Introduction
to
Coin Investment

A Rare Dime

In 1894 at the San Francisco Mint a rarity was created: the 1894-S dime. During the preceding year, 1893, nearly 2½ million were produced at this western mint. During the following year, 1895, the dime mintage exceeded one million. What happened in 1894? Only 24 pieces—yes, just 24 in all—were struck! Thus one of America's most famous classic rarities came to be.

The reason for striking just 24 pieces is not known today. One account has it that 24 pieces, amounting to $2.40 in face value, were struck in order to balance the coining account ledgers for that year. Another theory—and this is probably the most reasonable—is that 24 impressions were struck in order to test the dies. The anticipation at that time was that many more, perhaps over a million, would be issued. When no further coinage order was forthcoming the mintage remained at just 24 pieces. Of those 24 pieces fewer than 12 are known to exist today.

My first encounter with an 1894-S dime was in 1957. James F. Ruddy, who was to become my coin business partner in 1958, purchased on my behalf a mint-condition specimen for $4,750.00 at an auction sale. $4,750.00 for a dime! This news, sensational at the time, was quickly spread all over America by the various newspaper wire services. The result was a deluge of thousands and thousands of letters and postcards! I appeared on NBC's 'Today' TV show as a result of this dime purchase.

What happened to the 1894-S dime? It was sold within a month or two into one of America's finest private collections, that of Hon. and Mrs. R. Henry Norweb.

Another 1894-S dime came my way in 1961. Dealer Abe Kosoff offered at auction the collection formed by Edwin Hydeman. The coin was described in part: "Although there were supposed to have been 24 coins struck, there seem to be only 7 known specimens of the 1894-S dime. All are gems in Proof condition. The present market for rarities of this caliber should result in a runaway price for this offering. So seldom does it appear, that advanced collectors would best reach for the 1894-S now."

James F. Ruddy and I were contemplating buying the coin for our own company stock. What would it bring? The last known record was $4,750.00 for the 1894-S dime we purchased in 1957. Now in 1961 it was four years later—and as the coin market has a way of doing, prices in general had advanced. $8,000? $10,000? Just before the sale we received a telephone call from a prominent New York industrialist. He *had* to own that dime—and he wanted us to buy it for him! A few hours before the sale was to take place I received my instructions in the form of a coded telegram. There was a ripple of excitement on the sale floor as the bidding progressed: from the opening bid up to $11,500, then to $11,750, then to $12,000. There was a pause, and then the price continued upward: $12,250, $12,500, on to $12,750, and then the final bid to me: $13,000. The coin was mine!

The $13,000 was described as a "runaway price," and again the 1894-S dime created a sensation.

However, yesterday's "runaway price" is often tomorrow's bargain. I have seen this happen time and time again in the coin business. So, in 1972 at the American Numismatic Association convention an 1894-S dime sold for nearly $50,000. In 1974 James F. Ruddy and I resold the same piece for nearly $100,000.

Q. David Bowers, author of this book, has been an advocate of rare coin investment for many years— long before there was a widespread interest in the subject. His firm, Bowers and Ruddy Galleries, has made fortunes in this field for many of its clients.

A few of the many Bowers and Ruddy Galleries catalogues of the recent years.

Forecasting the Future

In two decades of numismatics my business partner James F. Ruddy and I have seen fortunes made in coin investment. We have helped many people make vast sums. We have seen a lot happen—all of it interesting, and much of it providing a lesson to follow.

There is much written—now and in the past—in the name of "coin investment." Some of this is thoughtful and meaningful. Other information is not worth the paper it is printed on. During many years of writing articles and publications on rare coins (for *Coin World, Numismatic News, Numismatic Scrapbook Magazine, The Encyclopedia Americana,* and *Reader's Digest*—just to mention a few places where my writings have appeared in print) I have endeavored to be objective, honest, and to present all sides of the story.

So it was with pleasure that I read the introduction to Harry J. Forman's book, *How You Can Make Big Profits Investing in Coins.* Mr. Forman said: "Anyone can make predictions, and if he does so in a field in which he is already well-known, they are sure to be widely read. Moreover, by waiting until people's memories have become somewhat blurred, and then republishing only his successes, he can often build up a rather good reputation for himself.

"In the numismatic field we have three kinds of forecasters. The first and commonest is the person who makes predictions simply as a promotional device to help sell whatever he has on hand. I don't say that in all, or even most cases, this involves a deliberate deception. On the contrary, the very fact that a person has invested his own money to purchase one or another item would indicate a certain amount of faith in its market potential. But such predictions necessarily lack true discrimination and depend for their success, if not on luck, then on the progress of the market as a whole.

"A second type of forecaster is the non-professional numismatist who dabbles in speculation and writes books or articles on market trends. Such an individual is more serious

Above: Q. David Bowers and James F. Ruddy are shown with the United States Mint 1792 coining press exhibit at the American Numismatic Association convention several years ago.

Right: Don Suter. Over the years Don Suter has headed the Investment Department of Bowers and Ruddy Galleries and has supervised the investment "portfolios" of many individual investors, pension plans, profit-sharing funds, and others. Working with over thirty Bowers and Ruddy Galleries staff members he has given investors with the firm first pick from the many magnificent collections the firm has handled.

in his selections and understands that there are always widespread differences in the potential of various issues and series. But for all that, his livelihood is not dependent on his predictions, and even should they fail he is still reimbursed by his royalties.

"The third and rarest type is the successful full-time dealer who forecasts not for promotional purposes, but simply to share his insights with the general investing public. My good friend Q. David Bowers is one such forecaster, having given much excellent investment advice through the *Empire Review* and more recently the *Rare Coin Review* [Bowers and Ruddy Galleries, Inc.]."

Before turning away from Mr. Forman's nice words I might mention something which I consider to be significant: *I was the only dealer specifically mentioned by Mr. Forman in his introduction.*

It is my hope in this book to provide you with some soundly-based information which will enable you to intelligently and profitably invest in rare coins. Read this book carefully and I believe that it will pay for itself many, many times over. I might mention at this point that I offer no get-rich-quick formula (nor would any responsible and experienced professional numismatist offer such a thing) nor is coin investment absolutely foolproof.

Past Success

Over the years our firm has helped build some of the finest collections in America and Europe. Without exception, to my knowledge, anyone who has had us assemble for him a choice collection or collection/investment group of American coins and who has held it for five years or more has made a nice profit upon selling it. I believe that this is a rather remarkable statement—and it is one that few other sellers and few other investment fields can match.

While profits are certainly possible in week-to-week or month-to-month trading, unless you have the time to keep

Rare Coins at Auction!

$16,000

$16,000

$6,800

$17,000

$7,500

$4,600

A rare coin auction is always an exciting event! Over the years the author and his firm have catalogued some of the most important numismatic properties ever sold on the auction block. Above are shown some of the prizes from the Terrell Collection Sale (May 1973), and a scene from the event itself: auctioneer George Bennett saying "Sold!"

right on top of the market it would seem that the most consistent profits are made by purchasing choice coins and putting them away for a number of years. At least this has been the case in the past. Also to be remembered is the fact that the dealer's margin of profit or sales commission might well use up any profit made on a short term basis. However, on a long term basis this diminishes in importance.

As a dealer I have seen thousands of collectors and collector-investors enter the market, stay for a short while or possibly for a long time, and then sell their coins. I have also seen thousands of investors plunge into the coin market quickly without taking the time to check the market situation or, for that matter, to even learn about numismatic publications and the offerings of other coin dealers. It has been my experience that the collectors and collector-investors have done the best! To this I attribute the knowledge possessed by the collector and collector-investor.

It is very difficult to enter coins blindly as an investor and do well without knowing much about what you are buying and without being aware of the coin market. (I mention the latter factor, for hardly a month goes by without some new firm advertising itself as "one of the largest in the business," etc. running large and impressive advertisements in financial journals. Having seen some of the "investments" sent to the customers of such firms, I can only feel sorry for their customers.) It continually amazes me how many investors will spend large sums on coins without taking the trouble to learn even the most basic facts about coins and the coin market.

Don't let this happen to you! While you are buying coins, or before you buy coins, learn something about them. Hopefully this book will be a major step in this direction for you. Persons who have made the most consistent profits have been those who have known the most.

History
of the
Coin Investment
Market

Chapter 2
History of the Coin Investment Market

The Early Years

The beginning of the coin business in the United States dates from the mid-1850's, during which time several persons became full-time or part-time coin dealers. One Edward Cogan claimed to have been the very first, his interest having been whetted by the discontinuance of the United States large cents and half cents and the coming of the new and smaller copper-nickel flying eagle cents in 1857.

Prior to this time the hobby of coin collecting was limited to only a few dozen numismatists in the United States. American coins were worth very little over face value. The main sources for coins were bankers and bullion dealers who, when alerted to watch for scarce dates, would pick them out and sell them to collectors for a modest premium.

The United States Mint at Philadelphia was actively forming its collection (presently housed in the Smithsonian Institution) during the 1840's and 1850's. The mint actively bought, sold, and traded coins. Several trays of old coins—particularly large cents of the previous few decades—were kept on hand for this purpose. Collectors desiring specific dates could often obtain them for face value or for a modest premium. The few collectors who were interested in coins during this period—collectors such as J.J. Mickley and Matthew Stickney—were able to assemble extensive collections for a moderate cost. For instance, in the year 1827 J.J. Mickley obtained four Proof 1827 quarters from the Philadelphia Mint and paid just face value for the four pieces!

In 1962 a single 1827 quarter from this original Mickley group of four sold for nearly $15,000! Today it would be worth even more—probably in the $50,000 range.

The American Numismatic Society was founded in 1858. By 1860 there were several other societies, a handful of coin dealers, and several hundred coin collectors in the United States.

The years from approximately 1860 to 1866 saw the first "boom" in the coin market. The most active series and the series in greatest demand by nearly everyone (including the U.S. Mint, which was one of the most active "dealers" at the time) comprised medals of George Washington. In a period when a choice 1793 large cent (now worth over $1,000) could be purchased for $10 certain scarce Washington medals would be bid up in furious competition to $100 or $500 or even more! Also in vogue were medallic portraits of Admiral Vernon, Lafayette, and Benjamin Franklin—to mention just a few of the more popular figures.

The next few decades were formative years in American numismatics. Investors as such in coins were unknown. Most coin owners were numismatists. Indeed, they had to be—as a degree of numismatic knowledge was certainly necessary to intelligently buy the favorite series of the day, series such as medals, United States colonial coins, tokens and store cards, and early American half cents and large cents.

Coins increased in value gradually. A 1793 cent which sold for $7.50 in 1866 might sell for $15.00 in 1875, $25.00 in 1885, and $30.00 by 1890. Many collectors considered their holdings to be good investments, but investment per se was not the main consideration.

Collecting during these formative years had its problems, just as it does today. Forgeries lay in wait for the unwary, and the grading habits of collectors and dealers sometimes sparked controversy.

However, unlike today there was very little interest in collecting coins from the various United States branch mints.

The presence of a "CC" (for Carson City, Nevada—a mint operated from 1870 through 1893) or an "S" (for the San Francisco Mint which was established in 1854) on a coin attracted little interest. In fact, there was no catalogue or guide listing which mintmarks were available! This seems incredible in view of today's values attached to certain rarities bearing these tiny mintmarks.

The 1890's

By 1890 there were dealers in most cities in the eastern part of the United States. Boston, New York City, and Philadelphia became the central points. J.W. Scott, W. Elliott Woodward, the auction firm of Bangs, Merwin & Co., the Chapman Brothers of Philadelphia, John Haseltine, Lyman H. Low, Ed Frossard, and Charles Steigerwalt were among the leading dealers of that day.

Early in the 1890's a number of important things happened. The American Numismatic Association was formed in 1891, thus providing a common meeting place for the exchange of ideas and values among collectors from all parts of the United States and elsewhere. *The Numismatist,* which began publication in 1888, was adopted as the official American Numismatic Association journal. Today the ANA, as it is popularly called, ranks as the world's largest and most important non-profit organization devoted to the furtherance of numismatics.

About the same time A.G. Heaton, a professional artist by trade and a numismatist by avocation, published a treatise on coins from the United States branch mints. This popular booklet was distributed by coin dealers everywhere and gave momentum to the collecting of coins by mintmark varieties. Today such collecting is an inseparable part of numismatics. No less important was the publication and wide circulation by J.W. Scott in 1893 of the *Standard Catalogue,* the first generally-used guide to coin values in America.

In 1893 the main topic of conversation in the United States was the Columbian Exposition in Chicago. Numismatically the world's fair was very active, with the firm of J.W. Scott having two separate coin sales displays and with numerous other collectors, dealers, and museums participating. The event also saw the distribution of the first commemorative coins issued by the United States: the 1892 and 1893 Columbian half dollars and the 1893 Isabella quarter, all of which heightened the public's interest in coins.

There was considerable interest in the new Columbian halves and Isabella quarters. Many thousands were sold at the fair, but quantities remained unsold after the event ended. Following the fair closing, one syndicate offered to buy 100,000 Columbian half dollars from the United States Treasury, provided that any additional unsold pieces be melted by the government. This proposal was rejected, and large quantities of unsold half dollars were released into circulation at face value.

1893 Isabella quarters fared a bit better as an investment medium. These pieces were originally sold for $1 each, but due to the fact that for the same price a Columbian half dollar could be purchased (and human nature dictated that a 50-cent piece would be a better value than a 25-cent piece at the same price) and also because the Isabella quarters were quietly distributed (the half dollars, in contrast, were promoted with large displays) the quarters were poorly received at the time of issue. The unsold pieces were then wholesaled to coin dealers for a nominal premium above face value. These quarters were called a "good investment" by many, and words to this effect even appeared editorially in the American Numismatic Association's journal, *The Numismatist*. The price rose to $1.50 per coin, but the supply was too great for the demand at the time, and the price dropped to a lower level. Those who had the foresight to weather the price drop were able to sell large quantities for $2.50 to $5.00 per coin in the 1920's and 1930's, and this is precisely what several dealers and investors did. Today, of course, the $5.00 price seems in retrospect to be an incredible bargain.

Leading Numismatic Organizations

The American Numismatic Association, organized in 1891, is the world's leading non-profit numismatic organization. Q. David Bowers (ANA Life Member 336) and James F. Ruddy (ANA Life Member 337) would be pleased to send you complete membership information. "The Numismatist," published monthly, is a source for information, offerings, and other items of interest. Two long-ago issues from 1909 are shown above.

The two leading dealers' organizations are the Professional Numismatists Guild and its worldwide counterpart, the International Association of Professional Numismatists. Dealer members are bound by a rigid code of ethics.

The Early 20th Century

By the early part of the 20th century there was a great interest in all American coins—from colonial issues to gold pieces. Collectors belatedly learned that many Liberty seated and earlier coins were really rare in top condition as no one had the foresight to save them in quantity when they were available for face value. Rarities emerged on the scene, with values of $1,000 to $5,000 per coin being attached to such items as the 1804 silver dollar, 1822 half eagle ($5 gold piece), 1787 Brasher doubloon, and a few others. It was announced that $10,000.00 each had been paid by a private collector for two $50 pattern gold coins of 1877. (Note: these coins, now permanently in the Smithsonian Institution Collection, would probably bring several hundred thousand dollars each if sold today.)

The term "investment" came into use in the coin market and was mentioned in print many times. Coins were indeed a good investment, and while not all items increased in value, the collector or investor having diverse holdings almost always realized an attractive profit over cost when his collection was sold.

The 1930's

By present-day standards the coin business was an infant in the years before 1934. Most allied fields of endeavor such as rare books, Currier & Ives prints, and art shared in the stock market boom of the 1920's. Not so with coins. Collecting and investing in coins was limited to a select few thousand persons, and coin values in this period increased steadily but not spectacularly or unnaturally.

Coin prices did not spiral with the stock market rise of the 1920's, so when the day of reckoning came for the stock market, coins held their values well. There were some exceptions. Some of the higher-priced issues (such as territorial gold pieces) softened in price somewhat, but the structure as a whole remained firm.

Beginning in 1934-1935 the coin market entered a tremendous growth period. The early commemorative half dollars of this era—issues such as the Maryland, Hudson, Spanish Trail, Connecticut, and others—gave impetus to the growing market.

Spurred on by dealers' advertisements and news releases and by the reluctance of collectors and investors to part with what they owned during a rising market, the Spanish Trail half dollars rose in value to $4.00 and then to $6.00 each (today they are worth several hundred dollars apiece). What really started the commemorative boom, however, was the 1935-D and S Boone set—the rare variety with small "1934" in the field. Only 2,000 of these sets were struck. A premature eastern news release resulted in nearly the entire issue being sold to speculators. When the official issuing commission announcement appeared in *The Numismatist* and other publications the coins had long since been sold. The price jumped immediately to $50.00 per set!

In 1936 commemorative half dollars were the main topic of conversation everywhere. Most of the new issues were quickly oversubscribed, often with the supply being rationed at the time of distribution. The Rhode Island Tercentenary issue (totaling 50,000 coins) was sold out in a matter of *hours* after the coins were first placed on sale. The 1936 P-D-S (for Philadelphia, Denver, and San Francisco) Cincinnati half dollars jumped immediately from the issue price of $7.75 per set to $25.00 per set, then to $35.00, and then to $50.00. Thousands of dollars of profit were made by collectors, investors, and dealers. Many pages of *The Numismatist, The Numismatic Scrapbook Magazine,* and other publications of this time and the next two years were crammed with advertisements for commemorative half dollars. A new crop of dealers was born: dealers specializing in commemoratives. The first large speculative market in coins was on its way.

The commemorative market of the 1935-1939 years would be an interesting book in itself. In my *Coins and Collectors* book (published in 1964) I devoted a chapter to this market phenomenon.

By 1939 the bloom was gone from the rose. Interest waned. Large quantities of commemorative half dollars remained unsold, and many were returned to the mint for melting. Others were sold to dealers and investors at large discounts from the original issue premium price. By 1939 Cincinnati sets had dropped in price from a high of $50.00 to just $15.00 to $17.50 per set, and no one was in a hurry to buy them.

The price structure of the 1936 P-D-S Cincinnati set is typical of many of these issues. In 1936 the official issue price of the set of three pieces ($1.50 face value) was $7.75. By late 1936 and early 1937 the price had risen to $50.00 per set. In 1939 the price dropped to just $16.00 per set as the speculative fever waned. By 1944 the price had inched upward to about $17.00 per set. By 1949 the price was $25.00. By 1954 the value doubled to $55.00. In 1959 the price had climbed to $95.00. By 1963 the figure was $325.00. In 1974 the price was over $750. This price analysis says, in essence, that an investor buying in at the peak of the market in 1936-1937 had to wait 15 years or more to break even, but as a long term investment an attractive profit was shown. An investor buying in at the beginning of the market could have shown a profit any time since the original purchase. An investor buying at the slump years of the market (in this instance 1939 to 1944) could have shown a profit in any of the successive years.

The information just stated is of a purely factual nature. The Cincinnati example is representative. Other issues did about the same. Anyone interested in the long-term price behavior of commemorative half dollars can find ample research material by looking through catalogues, price lists, and publications of the past 30 to 40 years.

Our illustration just given, the Cincinnati set, is basically a scarce numismatic item. Only 5,000 sets were issued—a very

United States Commemorative Silver Coins

1900 Lafayette Silver Dollar

1893 Isabella Quarter

From 1892 to 1954 commemorative silver coins were issued in a wide variety of designs. With the exception of the 1893 Isabella quarter dollar and the 1900 Lafayette silver dollar, all United States commemorative coins of this period are half dollars. The 1928 Hawaiian, 1937 Antietam, and 1927 Vermont issues, three of 48 major designs produced over the years, are shown on this page—together with the 1893 Isabella quarter and Lafayette silver dollar.

Events commemorated on coins range from the significant to the obscure. Among the former coins are the 1892 and 1893 Columbian Exposition, 1935 Connecticut tercentenary (300th anniversary), 1946 Iowa statehood centennial, and the 1915 Panama Pacific International Exposition. Among the lesser events from a national viewpoint are the 1936 300th anniversary of York County in Maine, the 1786-1936 anniversary of the Lynchburg, Virginia city charter, and the 150th anniversary of the founding of the city of Hudson in New York state.

1928 Hawaiian Half Dollar

1937 Antietam Half Dollar

1927 Vermont Half Dollar

low mintage for a popular modern United States coin. The price slumped in 1939 because of several reasons. The price rose sharply at the beginning. Non-numismatists (i.e., pure speculators) who had sets kept a watchful eye on the price structure. As soon as it leveled off and the "WE WANT TO BUY COMMEMORATIVES" type of advertisements became fewer and fewer, the speculators sold their sets and took a quick profit. Another factor was the number of collectors interested in a Cincinnati set at the $50.00 price level. *All coin investment is predicated on the assumption that there will sometime be a demand for a particular set or collection on the part of the collector,* who represents the ultimate consumer from an economic viewpoint. This is a very, very important precept to remember—and it is one that many investors tend to overlook.

Although 5,000 sets is a low mintage, there were not 5,000 collectors in 1939 interested enough in Cincinnati sets to pay $50.00 each or even more. The true value of the Cincinnati set was more nearly $15.00 to $17.00, the "bottoming out" price. From this low figure the price rose steadily, a rise based upon the increasing number of collectors who desired sets. Thus when the Cincinnati set broke the $50.00 mark again in 1953-1954 the $50.00 figure at that time was a solid and stable valuation. There were enough collectors in 1953 so that the supply and demand curves equated themselves at the $50.00 mark. In the years since 1953 the number of collectors has increased perhaps ten to twenty times. Thus today's price of nearly a thousand dollars per set would seem to be solidly based.

The commemorative market of the late 1930's, although it may have hurt a few unwise investors who purchased their holdings at the top of the market, had a tremendously favorable effect on numismatics. It introduced thousands of people to coin collecting. Some left coins in a hurry when the market fell, but thousands stayed on and benefited greatly.

Other things were happening in the coin market during the 1930's. In the early part of the decade you could have purchased an Uncirculated 1909-S V.D.B. cent (a rare Lincoln cent now worth several hundred dollars) for 25c, or a roll of 50 pieces for just 25c per coin, for that matter. By the end of the decade these coins sold for $2 to $3 each.

1885 Proof Liberty nickels (now worth several hundred dollars each) were a 25c item in the 1930's; a $1 to $2 item later in the decade. Similar price rises were taking place in other series—Indian cents, Washington quarters, half dollars, gold coins, and so on. While many investors bemoaned their commemorative market losses, the irrefutable fact remains that if they had diversified their holdings and had purchased some Lincoln cents, Liberty standing quarters, and other coins as well their investment taken as a whole would have shown a spectacular profit! This is the old "don't have all of your eggs in one basket" axiom.

Of great importance to the coin market were several other happenings during the 1930's. Wayte Raymond, a prominent New York City coin dealer, published the *Standard Catalogue*. Prior to the Raymond effort the only reference books in general use were the J.W. Scott catalogues (which were last revised in 1913!) and the Guttag Brothers catalogues of the mid-1920's. The *Standard Catalogue* was issued on a regular basis with frequent new editions. Containing up-to-date prices, interesting information, and excellent illustrations the various editions were distributed far and wide. Until the advent of the postwar *Guide Book of United States Coins* the *Standard Catalogue* had the popular price guide field to itself. The *Standard Catalogue* educated collectors and investors alike. Prior to its appearance even information concerning recent United States coins was sketchy at best. Several years before, a collector wrote to the editor of *The Numismatist* and asked whether any Lincoln cents had been struck at the Philadelphia Mint in 1922. The editor didn't know and asked help from readers. This lack of knowledge was not unusual; few other people knew the answer either.

It was Wayte Raymond, by the way, who published one of the first advertisements specifically featuring the investment appeal of rare coins. In 1912 his firm, the United States Coin Company, advertised in *The Numismatist* (we quote the first part of his advertisement): "COINS AS AN INVESTMENT. Many harsh words are said about collectors who interest themselves in a natural speculation as to whether or not the coins they are buying today will have appreciated in value ten years from now. Numismatists of the old school tell us that the true collector is not interested in any such appreciation in the value of his collection but derives his entire profit and pleasure from the coins while in his hands. We feel, however, that the average American collector while he greatly enjoys his coins also feels very pleased if on disposing of his collection he realizes a profit . . ."

Another important event during the 1930's was the production by the Whitman Publishing Company of its first so-called "Penny Boards," which were cardboard coin albums for Lincoln cents. These boards were widely distributed among the public. Many historians today agree that these popular boards were the major factor in the subsequent emphasis on collecting 20th century coins by dates and mintmarks. By means of these inexpensive boards thousands of people entered the field of coin collecting.

There were many other influences during the 1930's. Dealer B. Max Mehl of Fort Worth, Texas spent hundreds of thousands of dollars each year publicizing his coin business. Advertisements for his *Star Rare Coin Encyclopedia* appeared in major magazines and newspapers everywhere. At one point Mehl even had his own nationwide radio program! People began to look through their pocket change. While they might not have found a valuable 1913 Liberty nickel (the main coin for which Mehl advertised nationwide), they did develop an interest in coin collecting.

Another important influence was the *Numismatic Scrapbook Magazine*. Starting from a small beginning in 1935 editor Lee Hewitt built this publication up to be a favorite of thousands of collectors everywhere. M.L. Beistle, Wayte Raymond, and others marketed albums with celluloid slides which provided convenient coin storage for advanced collectors. (Plastic holders and polyethylene coin envelopes, popular for storing coins today, did not come into general use until the 1950's.) The number of coin collectors increased during the 1930's, and by 1940 nearly every large city in the United States had one or more full-time coin dealers.

The 1940's

During the period from 1940 to 1950 the modern structure of coin prices began to take form. Whereas all Proof Liberty nickels, for example, had been priced all about the same during the 1930's, a different price structure emerged during the 1940's. Figures taken from the 1934 and 1949 editions of the *Standard Catalogue* show this dramatically: In Proof condition nickels had the following values in 1949: 1884 $10, 1885 $25, 1886 $10, 1887 $4.40, and 1888 $4.50. Fifteen years earlier in 1934 each of these coins catalogued precisely 50c each!

The "key" dates such as 1885 and 1886 became more valuable than the others. In other series 1877 Indian cents, 1909-S V.D.B. Lincoln cents, 1916-D dimes, 1932-D and S quarters, and other scarcities became the varieties most in demand. Collectors started looking through millions of coins in circulation. A new price structure emerged: the prices of coins in a given series increased in direct proportion to their scarcity in circulation.

As prices rose, coins in "Good" and "Very Good" condition became valuable if they were scarce dates. Previously, a 20th century coin in any grade less than "Extremely Fine" or "Uncirculated" was fit only for spending. Early editions of the *Standard Catalogue* priced coins only in Uncirculated and Proof grades! It was soon learned, however, that there were just not enough Uncirculated and Proof coins to go around as the number of collectors doubled and tripled, and then doubled and tripled again. Circulated coins of scarce dates were sought eagerly.

Immediately following World War II a new colossus appeared on the numismatic scene: the *Guide Book of United States Coins*, authored by Richard S. Yeoman and printed by the Whitman Publishing Company. With the vast and varied distributive outlets of Whitman the *Guide Book* was an immediate success. Today in the 1970's it ranks as one of the most popular books ever published on any subject in America. Over ten million copies have been sold!

During the 1940's coin prices rose sharply. A survey of great auction sales of the 1940-1950 years (Dunham, Higgy, World's Greatest Collection, Hall, Bell, Flanagan, Atwater, Neil, etc. sales) shows a sharp increase in the price of nearly everything from half cents to double eagles. The number of new collectors continued to increase while the supply of coins remained constant, hence the inevitable price rise. The inflationary postwar economy contributed also.

This price increase was a healthy one. There were minor adjustments in certain series from time to time, but the long term trend was upward.

The 1950's

In 1950 the Philadelphia Mint announced that it would resume the production of Proof sets. Earlier, Proof coins had been sold to collectors from 1858 through 1916 inclusive and then from 1936 through 1942. Coinage was suspended after 1942 and was not resumed until 1950, as noted.

In 1950 the Philadelphia Mint produced 51,386 Proof sets. In 1951 57,500 sets were made. As production climbed year by year there began to be considerable interest in Proof sets from an investment viewpoint, but the interest was limited. We remember James Incorporated, rare coin dealers of Louisville, Kentucky, showing us a nice "thank you letter" they received from the mint in appreciation for their particularly large 1951 Proof set order! The years when millions of sets were to be produced and when ordering quantities would be restricted were yet to come.

Two American Rarities

The 1876-CC twenty-cent piece shown above (actual size and also an enlargement) was sold by Bowers and Ruddy Galleries in the Armand Champa Collection sale of May 1972. The specimen, choice Uncirculated, was formerly owned by noted American composer Jerome Kern. At the Armand Champa sale it fetched $24,000. In 1974 we offered the buyer a generous profit, advertised it for $59,000, and received four orders for the coin!

The 1884 trade dollar, one of just ten specimens believed minted of this date, is from the fabulous Robert Marks Collection handled by Bowers and Ruddy Galleries in 1972. From 1953 to 1977 we handled six specimens of this, one of America's most famous rarities.

In 1950 the Denver Mint produced only 2,630,030 nickels—the smallest nickel mintage since 1931. When the mintage figures were released, excitement prevailed! By May, 1951 a $2-face-value roll of 40 coins was selling for three times face, or $6. One dealer in the May, 1951 issue of the *Numismatic Scrapbook Magazine* said: "1950-D Nickels. Hectic! Write for prices." Still there was no great widespread interest in modern coins. Sample retail prices of modern coins selected from that 1951 *Scrapbook* issue show offerings at tiny fractions of what the same coins or sets would sell for today:

In 1951 a set of Lincoln cents in Brilliant Uncirculated grade and dated from 1934 to 1950 inclusive cost all of $2.50. A set of Jefferson nickels from 1938 to 1950 cost $8.50, and a set of Washington quarters in the same grade from 1932 through 1950 cost $77.50. A roll of 40 pieces of 1938-S quarters brought $35.00, and a roll of 1946-S quarters brought $11.00. A roll (20 pieces) of 1949 Philadelphia half dollars fetched $10.65, and a roll of the previously-mentioned low-mintage 1950-D nickels could be yours for as low as $5.10 if 50 or more rolls were bought.

In 1951 prices of individual rare coins were equally low in comparison to today's prices. A 1916 Brilliant Uncirculated Liberty standing quarter could be bought for just $85.00, or less than 1/15th of today's price. A 1917 Type I Brilliant Uncirculated quarter fetched $2.50 (now the coin sells for about $250). A 1909-S V.D.B. cent in Brilliant Uncirculated grade brought $10.50 (vs. about $300 now), and a 1931-S cent in the same grade cost $1.25 (vs. $45 to $50 now). There are many other examples.

In 1952 a new publication, the *Numismatic News,* was started in Iola, Wisconsin by Chester Krause. It proved to be very popular, and over a period of years it introduced thousands of new people to the field of coins. Meanwhile the American Numismatic Association was gaining thousands of new members, and the *Numismatic Scrapbook Magazine* was likewise gaining thousands of new subscribers. All of these new collectors wanted coins, and coin prices continued to rise. This price rise was well-founded and solidly based.

Not all collectors could have sets of Proof Liberty nickels (even if all Proof Liberty nickels ever coined were still in existence there would be only 1,475 sets possible) or sets of Uncirculated Indian cents—there simply were not enough coins to go around. Accordingly, a strong demand for modern sets such as Jefferson nickels, Roosevelt dimes, and Franklin half dollars developed.

By the end of 1955 the coin market was in the midst of a strong price rise. Conventions, once a scholarly gathering of numismatists, were proudly chalking up record attendances as hundreds of newcomers and beginning collectors visited these large affairs to see what coin collecting was all about.

Attracted by the stories of price rises, investors began to flock to the marketplace. The previously small market in rolls and Proof sets grew rapidly. A 1936 Proof set, a group of coins which sold for $100 in 1954, reached a new level of $300. The prices of all other Proof sets dated 1936-1956 rose also. In mid-1956 a 1956 Proof set, although still available from the Mint for the issue price of $2.10 per set (note: issue prices have risen since then), commanded a price of $2.50 or so on the numismatic market. A record 669,384 sets were struck in 1956, nearly doubling the preceding year's total and exceeding over a dozen times the number struck in 1950, six years earlier.

The market in Proof sets continued to rise during the second half of 1956 and the first part of 1957. The 1936 Proof set, which had previously advanced to $300, went on to $550 and then to $600. Other sets found ready buyers at new levels also. Every day more and more people desired them, so it seemed.

Late in 1957 the market for Proof sets fell. The 1936 set dropped back to $300, and other modern issues retreated to lower levels. Again, in 1957 those who were "hurt" by the drop of prices were those who had ALL of their holdings in Proof sets. *Those who diversified fared well.* During the same time that modern Proof sets fell, dealers were posting new high buying prices for 19th century coins and scarcer 20th century issues. The coin market taken in its entirety was stronger than ever!

Many of the newcomers who were introduced to coins with the 1956-1957 bull market in Proof sets stayed with coins and went on to build collections or to invest in other numismatic series. The number of collectors continued to grow.

1958 and 1959 were good years for the collector, investor, and dealer alike. Anyone who purchased Proof sets at the reduced prices of those years would have no trouble doubling or tripling his investment capital within the next five years. Likewise, anyone who bought Lincoln cents, half cents and large cents, colonial coins, early gold coins, $5,000 rarities, $5 common-date Liberty nickels, or what have you, would show a very attractive three to five year long term profit.

1960 saw the inception of the publication *Coin World*. Beginning with its first issue, coin prices were available to collectors everywhere on a *weekly* basis. The market became more volatile and active. Within four years the circulation of *Coin World* climbed past the 100,000 mark. There were few secrets in the coin business now. Especially with actively traded modern coins everyone was up-to-date on the latest prices.

In the early 1960's the United States Treasury Department released to the public hundreds of millions of dollars worth of early silver dollars, mostly issues dated from 1878 through 1904. The appearance of scarce dates in this hoard caused great public interest and brought thousands of new collectors into the numismatic field. American Numismatic Association membership applications increased dramatically as did the subscription rolls of popular numismatic magazines. The story was the same: the increasing number of collectors matched with a static supply of available coins forced prices upward.

In 1961-1962 the collecting of coins by design type—the formation of what are called *type sets*—took on new popularity. The introduction of the *Library of Coins* and Whitman *Bookshelf* albums provided an attractive and convenient way to store and display coins by types. Important type set coins such as the 1796 quarter, half dollars of 1796-1797, 1873-1874 silver coins with arrows at the date, 1917 Type I quarters, etc. doubled and tripled in value. James F. Ruddy and I were among the first to publish specific investment information pertaining to collecting coins by design types. Our recommendations published in 1963 in the *Empire Investors Report* were widely heeded at the time, as were later recommendations on the same subject written by us and published by *The Forecaster,* an independent investment advisory service.

By 1963 investment in certain modern rolls and bags of coins reached what one dealer called "epidemic proportions." It seemed that anything bright and shiny and of circular shape was being called a "good investment" by some advisors. Hoarding became so widespread that there developed a scarcity of new coins in circulation! The Treasury Department vowed to stop all of this speculation, and rather drastic measures were taken. Mintmarks were omitted on issues struck at branch mints from 1965 through 1967! The practice of strictly dating coins in the years in which they were produced—a practice which had been strictly adhered to for many decades—was also suspended for a while. The result of this was to end speculation and to dampen prices, at least for a few years.

It is strange to note that the government itself then did a complete reversal and decided to go into the coin business in a big way in the late 1960's. The government manner of doing this (the first Proof silver Eisenhower dollar issue was released at $10, a rather high price, rather than $2 or $3 — prices which would have also shown a nice profit for the government) caused considerable criticism. Much criticism was also voiced in various numismatic publications about unnecessarily high issue prices of Proof sets, thoughtless statements made by the government concerning the "investment" value of coins it sells, and so on. It is my personal opinion that the United States government should issue modern coins to collectors for nominal prices—and let any future price appreciation accrue to collectors and investors. Also, by doing this the government gives beginning collectors and those with limited budgets a chance to participate equally in new issues and to begin the numismatic hobby at low cost. But this is a different subject apart from the main theme of this book.

During the 1960's the market for scarce and rare early coins of proven numismatic value remained strong. As an example, such early issues as colonials, 18th and 19th century silver coins, early gold coins, and related issues never faltered (even a tiny bit!) in price when the Treasury efforts against collectors were in progress.

Collector demand tends to be stronger than investment demand, so the market for collectors' coins tends to be steadier. The question "why don't investors buy earlier coins all of the time?" is a natural one to ask at this point. There are several answers to this. The main answer is that *knowledge* is necessary to collect and to invest in earlier issues. There are two ways to do this: to learn about these issues yourself, or, second, to buy from experienced professional numismatists who can help you. However, many so-called "investment advisors" simply are not experienced professional numismatists, so the investor consulting such a source would not be exposed to the advantages of investing in coins of proven numismatic desirability. Such "advisors" often buy up the things that are easiest to accumulate in quantity and recklessly sell them as being "good investments." Coins of true scarcity and rarity are never available in quantity, so these are rarely "recommended."

My own personal opinion differs. As noted earlier, the most successful investor is the one who takes the time to learn about coins and the coin market. At Bowers and Ruddy

Galleries, Inc. James F. Ruddy and I have always recommended that our investment clients become acquainted with coins—and buy reference books, subscribe to numismatic publications, join the American Numismatic Association, and so on. We have done this in full confidence knowing that the coins we sell can stand up to close scrutiny and comparison to the offerings of other sellers. Unfortunately (both for the individual investor and for the good of numismatics as a whole) some types of "investment advisors" prefer that their clients read only their own literature and not become familiar with what is going on in the general numismatic marketplace. The disadvantages of this to the investor are obvious.

Recent Times

After moving "sideways" (as they say in the stock market) for several years, the coin market in general picked up again in the late 1960's and very early 1970's. At the same time the stock market was at a low ebb. Strangely enough, the price movements of stocks and coins do not appear to be related. When stocks are strong then coins usually are also strong, for there is a general "good feeling" in the investment market, and this extends to all investment media. Also to be considered as a factor is the spending of stock market profits on coin collections and coins for investment. When the stock market is weak, as it was in the 1969-1970 years and again in 1973-1974, then the coin market often is strong as investors' attention turns to more rewarding areas. Taken as a whole, investment in rare coins has sharply outpaced the Dow-Jones Industrial Averages, the most commonly-quoted index of stock market values.

Likewise, there does not seem to be much correlation between interest rates and coin investment. During 1972-1974, when commercial interest rates to large businesses were at unprecedentedly high levels, over 12% at one point, and when record high rates were being paid on certificates of deposit and on savings account deposits, one might think that tremendous amounts of money would have been channeled into banking areas and away from coins. The opposite was true. This marked one of the greatest boom times in modern numismatics! An explanation of this apparently contradictory phenomenon is that unusually high interest rates are symptomatic of rampant inflation, and, historically, investment in rare coins has been one of the best hedges against inflation possible.

The 1973-1974 years saw a great growth in interest in the rare coin field. During this time there was tremendous interest in gold. It was subsequently announced that for the first time since 1933 the American public could hold gold bullion—beginning on December 31, 1974. The popular press took a very bullish view of the situation and said that once gold bullion could be owned by the American public prices would soar. One of America's most respected economic experts predicted that the price of gold, then in the range of $150 per ounce, would soon go to $400 per ounce! Numerous other "authorities" suggested bullion prices of $200 to $400.

As December 31, 1974 was too long to wait, thousands of investors took a short cut by purchasing gold coins of high intrinsic value. Others bought rare gold coins believing that when gold bullion doubled or tripled in price, as it was certain to do after December 31, 1974, rarities would double and triple in price also (this thinking is fallacious, for if one pays, for example, $5,000 for a rare gold coin with an intrinsic value of $50, it doesn't make much difference whether the intrinsic value then doubles or triples—for the collector's value is so much higher). This gold "boom" spurred many artificial price increases.

During this frenzy of activity I told interested investors and collectors to be cautious—to stick with tried, true, and traditional items and not to jump on a bandwagon which, to me, seemed to have very weak supports.

Richard Buffum, columnist for the Los Angeles Times, interviewed coin dealers and others to ask their reaction to the coming "gold boom." I was a voice in the wilderness and instead of urging Los Angeles Times readers to spend their money as soon as possible on anything that was round and yellow, I urged caution, and even had the audacity to say that the gold boom would be a fizzle. I was the only one who did so.

December 31, 1974 came and went and gold bullion, which had nearly touched the $200 mark shortly before the magic date, didn't go to $400. In fact, it didn't even go to $300. In fact, it did something that it shouldn't have done: It dropped! With it dropped the value of quite a few gold coins and other items which were artificially inflated in price earlier. Later, in the autumn of 1976, the Los Angeles Times was to write a follow-up article on the subject—and I was pointed out as being the only person who correctly predicted several years earlier what would happen.

In the meantime, selected choice type coins—Indian cents, Liberty nickels, Barber coins, Liberty standing coins, and the like—increased in value.

Taken as a whole, recent years have been very excellent ones for the coin investor. The American economy appears to be strong, and the trend of inflation probably will continue inevitably upward. Prices of housing, real estate, of fuel and energy sources, transportation, and the like keep going up. In terms of spending power, money held in conservative investments such as savings account deposits in recent years has gone down. All of these factors should contribute to future strength in the coin market.

Several new factors are just beginning to be important. In recent years coins have been purchased by many far-seeing professional and business people as part of their participation in Keogh Plan accounts and I.R.A. accounts. Pension funds, investment institutions, and other money managers have investigated coins seriously and in many instances have acquired significant properties. In addition, the interest in coin investment, once mainly limited to collectors and investors in the United States has spread to other countries. For example, Bowers and Ruddy Galleries in 1971 advertised

1915-S Panama-Pacific commemorative sets for $12,500.00 each. We had several orders from Japan for these sets. (Our Japanese friends did well: now the sets are worth about $35,000.00 each!)

As more and more countries gain the affluence that has characterized the Unites States in recent decades then more and more numismatists will come into being around the world—and there will be a greater demand for *all* coins, including U.S. issues. It is now quite common for a numismatist in Germany, Japan, or Italy (to cite just a few examples) to desire to own a type set of U.S. gold or silver coins and other issues.

Few will question that coin investment has been spectacularly successful for those who have bought carefully and from responsible sources. So, all is well with the past. But what about the future? Perhaps this is best answered by quoting some comments I made in 1971 in an article in *The Forecaster*. I was discussing the 1902 Proof half dollar (although the comments would have been relevant for any other Proof Barber half dollar of the 1892-1912 years), a coin which sold for $80 in 1963 (when James F. Ruddy and I wrote our article on type coins for the *Empire Investors Report*) and which in 1971 sold for $180:

"Will the 1902 half dollar, a coin which might cost $180 today, be a good investment for the future? After all, quite a bit of profit has already been made by others on these coins—by people who bought them when they were cheaper ten years ago.

"This is a logical and reasonable question to ask. Perhaps the quickest way to answer would be to say that ten years ago isn't now, and that we must concern ourselves with the present, not the past. Valuable objects in any field—Rembrandt paintings, antiques, etc.—have a history of price appreciation over the years. Waiting to buy them for the prices of ten or twenty years ago is not realistic. So long as the trend of our economy is inflationary, prices seem to be headed for an ever-upward spiral. Coins have shared in this spiral and will continue to do so. Today (note: this was written in 1971) the number of available 1902 Proof half dollars combined with the number of people desiring them, have set the price at approximately $180. Again we remind our readers that we have picked the 1902 Proof half dollar merely as an example. The reasoning applies to many coins in the United States series."

As it turned out, the buyer of a Proof Barber half dollar for $180 in 1971 could have made a $100 profit by holding the coin for just one year and selling it in 1972! By 1977 the coin was worth over $700, and an even greater profit could be made!

Future Prospects

What about the future? In my opinion rare coins have an excellent future. The coin market itself is just beginning to be recognized as an important investment medium. Large investors such as profit-sharing programs and pension funds are just starting to move into the market. As knowledge of the past success of the coin investment field spreads, more and more people will be attracted to investment in choice and rare coins. The supply of older pieces remains static, so an upward price movement is the logical result.

Coins will be very much in the news in coming years. The 1776-1976 bicentennial coins created immense additional collector interest. Scarcely a week goes by without newspaper articles on the subject of modifying coin denominations or designs, interesting varieties and errors found in circulation, and the like. The United States Treasury Department in recent years has been taking an active interest in the coin collector. It is my prediction that the future will hold more commemorative and special issues in store.

On a worldwide scale, increasing inflation combined with more money in the hands of the average citizen will combine to increase interest in coins as a hobby and as an investment. Only a small part of the international potential has been tapped.

Yes, the years ahead will be good ones for coins. With planning you can share in the vast profits that are to come!

Chapter 3

Advantages

of

Coin Investment

As an investment medium coins have many advantages. Earlier I discussed how coin investment has proven itself in the past. Now I tell of some of the different aspects of investing in coins.

Easy Storage and Handling

Coins are small and are easy to store in a safe place. They require little if any special attention. A beautiful collection or investment group can be kept easily in a bank safe deposit box or vault.

In competition in 1971 James F. Ruddy and I made a bid for the Westwood Collection, one of the very finest collections of United States coins to come on the market in recent years. Our bid, a substantial one, was successful. The owner of the coins (who, incidentally, began collecting in 1953 and made a very substantial profit when he sold his holdings) kept his coins in a bank safe deposit box. His cost to store this magnificent group was a nominal sum, probably just a few dollars per year. The compactness of this stellar group of coins is perhaps best illustrated by noting that after the purchase was made I carried it to my office in a briefcase (after making proper insurance arrangements).

For most collectors and investors the bank safe deposit box is the best way to store coins over a long period of time. Insurance rates are much lower for coins kept this way; much lower than for coins kept in a home or other location.

Polyethylene envelopes, album pages with acetate slides, or small plastic holders are ideal for storing the coins. The only precaution to take is to be sure that the humidity or moisture level is not excessive. Should the bank vault be damp then a packet of silica gel put in the safe deposit box will absorb moisture. Or it might make good sense to put the coins in an airtight box or other container within the safe deposit box.

A low-amount insurance policy can be purchased through the American Numismatic Association (if you are a member) or through another source to cover coins in transit and while they are at your home or office for enjoyment, evaluation, or study. Such insurance is available for a nominal cost.

Coins are easily portable and can be carried from one place to another or sent through the mail. This makes the market for coins a worldwide one rather than just a local situation. As an example of the convenience of mail shipment I mention our purchase a few years ago of the Robert Marks Collection. I was able to ship a substantial percentage of the value of the collection—a group which included a magnificent Proof 1884 trade dollar, many Proof gold coins, and so on—back to the office in several small registered mail packets. It is the policy of many collectors and dealers to ship auction sale purchases and other particularly valuable acquisitions back home through the mail rather than to carry them personally. This is very convenient and represents a saving on insurance and handling.

Coins are Easy to Buy and Sell

In the field of selected quality coins the dealer's main problem is buying coins, not selling them. Rare and desirable coins are easy to sell—it is buying them that is difficult for the dealer. As a result, buying competition is intense among professional dealers, a situation which results in a higher price and a close-to-retail market value obtained by the collector or investor who sells. There is no "wholesale" market in the field of choice and rare coins. There is no opportunity for the dealer to say "please ship me ten Uncirculated 1862 silver

King of American Coins: The 1804 Silver Dollar

Above is shown the William Idler specimen of the famous 1804 United States silver dollar, a coin offered for $200,000.00 by Bowers and Ruddy Galleries in 1974. It is one of the highest-grade examples of this rarity. Dealer B. Max Mehl called the Idler 1804 "the best known specimen of this great rarity."

Describing another 1804, the Dunham Collection specimen sold in 1941, B. Max Mehl, America's leading dealer during the first half of the 20th century, told of the appeal that the 1804 silver dollar has to numismatists:

"In all the history of numismatics of the entire world there is not today and there never has been a single coin which was and is the subject of so much romance, interest, comment, and about which so much has been written and so much talked about and discussed as the United States silver dollar of 1804.

"While there may be coins of greater rarity (based upon the number of specimens known), no coin is so famous as the dollar of 1804! This is due to the fact that this great coin was the first coin of the United States mintage to have been recognized as the rarest coin of the United States from the very beginning of American numismatics more than one hundred years ago. And it is today, as it always has been, the best known and most sought-after coin, not only among collectors, but among the public in general as well."

The Idler specimen of the 1804 silver dollar has a long and illustrious pedigree which can be traced back more than a century! The roster of past owners of this rarity reads like a "who's who" of numismatics: William Idler, H.O. Granberg, William C. Atwater, William C. Atwater Family, Will W. Neil, Edwin Hydeman, Private Collection (the owner desired anonymity), World-Wide Coin Co., and Bowers and Ruddy Galleries.

Over the years the ownership of an 1804 dollar has automatically put its possessor in the front rank of famous numismatists. Whenever one of these "rarest of the rare" dollars comes on the market it is a numismatic landmark. The Bowers and Ruddy Galleries purchase of the 1804 silver dollar was attended by newspaper and television coverage all over the world!

dollars," for instance. A dealer must compete with collectors and other dealers for desirable pieces.

There are thousands of dealers who desire coins, so it is easy to quickly convert your coin holdings to cash. There is no waiting for your money. It is the policy of Bowers and Ruddy Galleries, Inc., for instance, to pay instant cash for all items purchased.

At this point I might mention that in twenty years in numismatics I have never seen a situation in which there was not extremely intense competition among dealers when a choice collection came up for sale. Any other leading professional dealer will verify this. *Never has there been a softness in the market for first-quality coins of proven rarity and value.*

In the coin market collectors and dealers all act independently. There is an orderly stream of collections being formed and later resold. Considering that there are hundreds of thousands of serious advanced collectors and millions of casual collectors (figures estimating as many as eight to ten million collectors have been published in recent years), the demand is stable and is not susceptible to sharp price fluctuations.

To illustrate this let me take as a random example a Proof 1870 Liberty seated silver dollar. There were 1,000 of these pieces coined over 100 years ago. If you take into consideration that various specimens have been lost or damaged over the years, then it is fairly safe to assume that probably 500 or 600 pieces survive today. It is further a safe assumption that few if any dealers have more than one or two pieces in stock, and most dealers have not even a single specimen.

Collectors who own 1870 Proof silver dollars have just a single coin. After all, why should they have two? Thus the available supply of 500 to 600 Proof pieces is spread out among many owners. Let us assume for purposes of illustration that this coin is worth an even $1,500 at the moment (the actual market price may be different at the time you read this; I pick $1,500 purely as an example). If you offer to pay $100 above the market the chances are excellent that you would not be able to buy more than a dozen pieces. In fact, even this estimate may be on the high side! Dealers who have 1870 Proof silver dollars will be happy to sell them to you, but why should the average collector spoil his set by picking out his prized 1870 and selling it separately?

On the other hand, should you have picked the 1870 Proof dollar as an investment ten years ago and should you have, say, two or three dozen by now, you would have no trouble selling them. There is sufficient demand by many collectors who would like an 1870 Proof silver dollar for their type sets or date sets to readily absorb such a small quantity. Or, virtually any dealer would be happy to buy them all as a lot, knowing full well that they could be sold quickly and easily. Thus the market in 1870 Proof silver dollars is stable. As the trend of coin prices moves upward, the price of 1870 silver dollars will move up with it. To the extent that the past may be an indication of the future I mention that the price of this coin 26 years ago (in 1948) was $45, a tiny fraction of what it is today. The 1870 Proof silver dollar is a relatively "safe" investment as the supply and demand are both widespread. Coins of this caliber can rightly be called "blue chips."

The market for your coins is an international one. Compare this, for instance, to real estate. If you purchase a piece of real estate on the wrong side of town and future growth doesn't happen to lie in that direction you are out of luck. In any event your real estate would generally appeal only to a buyer interested in purchasing land in your specific geographical location. On the other hand the market for coins is truly international. Your 1870 Proof silver dollar (to cite the example used earlier) appeals not only to the collector or investor in Oshkosh, Wisconsin, but to the buyer in Los Angeles or New York—or to the buyer in Tokyo, Copenhagen, or London, for that matter.

Standardized grading nomenclature and terminology have played an important part in this. Hence the simple listing

"1852 Original Proof half cent" was sufficient recently for Spink & Son, Ltd., prominent London dealers, to buy this coin from me—although they had not seen it previously and although I am located nearly half way around the world from them!

If another example is needed to illustrate how standard descriptions are useful to buyer and seller, I mention that when Yale University selected James F. Ruddy and me to purchase one of their coins—a Gem Proof example of the exceedingly rare MCMVII Extremely High Relief $20 gold piece—we were able to give an instant purchase decision simply by hearing a brief description of it over the telephone. When James F. Ruddy and I later sold the coin a similar brief description was all that was needed to consummate a sale with the new purchaser who was located 2,500 miles away! And so it goes with countless numismatic transactions, large and small, day in and day out.

Coins are Taxable at Low Rates

In most places around the world there is no property tax levied on a coin collection (as opposed, for instance, to real estate—where taxes seem to reach new highs each year). When time comes for you to sell your coins, profits are taxable at low capital gains rates (assuming you have held them for the minimum time required), with deductions allowed for expenses you have had during the course of acquiring your collection. Such expenses can include subscriptions to publications, memberships in numismatic organizations, postage, insurance, and even the cost of this book!

We might further mention that your coin collection is your own personal business and no one else's. Whether you have $10 worth of coins in your safe deposit box, $10,000 worth, or $100,000 worth is your business—and is not known by your neighbors or business associates. Assuming you do not choose to publicize your holdings, it is easy to "mind your own business" so far as the value of your coins is concerned. Your investment is a private matter.

On the romantic side of things there are many stories of fortunes being carried across international borders by secreting a few selected rare coins on one's person while fleeing to escape tyranny or some other threat. A selected group of rare coins can be a wonderful *private store of value.*

Coin Information is Readily Available

You do not have to be an expert to successfully invest in coins, although (as we have noted earlier) the more you learn about coins the greater your chances for investment success will be. Generally, coins are easy to identify and classify. Mintage figures, sales records, and price guides are available to assist you in your investment decisions—aiding you in the same way that earnings records, dividend information, industry projections, and other information is of use in the stock market.

When analyzing investment advice it is important to consider the source. Is the writer really familiar with rare coins? Is he an established professional with an excellent reputation in the industry? Analyze your information critically and objectively and then make your investment decision deliberately. *An established professional dealer is your best friend and advisor in this regard.* On the other hand, tipsters who promise "sure things" are here today and gone tomorrow.

Coins Have a Steady and Strong Market

Coin prices are not as volatile as are prices in many other investment media. With the exception of certain modern speculative issues, coin prices do not change on a day-to-day basis, but are more steady. The historical trend of rare coin prices has been upward. There are hundreds of different coins which have averaged a 10% to 25% or more per year price increase over the past few decades. Consider coins to be a long term investment. While individual factors vary, I would suggest a three to five year minimum period. In the past my customers who have shown the greatest profits have held coins for five to ten years or more.

What the coin market lacks in day-to-day price fluctuations it more than makes up in long-term movement. One of the main sources of coins for Bowers and Ruddy Galleries is buying from collectors and investors who purchased pieces years earlier from James F. Ruddy and me. Our customers have been very successful in the past. In the course of buying countless collections of United States coins over the years Jim Ruddy and I have never had a seller who has informed us of experiencing a loss when coins were held as a long term investment for five to ten years or more! We have purchased many coins from clients at five to ten times or more the prices they paid us when they acquired the coins in the 1950's or early 1960's. Indeed, the rare coin market has done *fantastically well* for those who have approached coin collecting and investing from a serious and well-reasoned viewpoint.

Coins are Interesting to Own and Collect

Coins are interesting to own as well as being a good investment. Coins provide infinite possibilities for historical appreciation. What stories coins could tell if only they could speak! But they remain silent—and therein lies a certain fascination. Perhaps your large cent of 1835 was owned by Abraham Lincoln when he was a struggling young lawyer. Was your 1883 nickel spent by a child for a souvenir at the Columbian Exposition in 1893? Was your 1852 gold double eagle once part of a buried treasure? Not knowing the answers to these questions makes the ownership of such pieces intriguing. Coins keep their secrets well!

Perhaps the story of Mr. Armand Champa, a fine gentleman and one of our firm's customers for many years, will illustrate the combined appeal of collecting and investment. During the 1960's Mr. Champa carefully built a choice collection. He subscribed to many different numismatic publications, ordered from a variety of dealers, attended coin conventions, and generally participated in the mainstream of numismatics. Whenever an important numismatic event took place, chances were that Armand Champa would be there!

A main function of the professional dealer is to furnish advice to his customers; advice in addition to selling coins. So it was with Armand Champa. Many times we would help him determine the rarity of a particular piece, help him decide whether he should "reach" to buy a piece now or whether he should wait for another which possibly might be offered for a slightly lower price later, and so on.

Although Mr. Champa's collection covered many different areas of American numismatics, he concentrated on United States pattern coins—a specialized field containing experimental, trial, and pattern pieces of various designs manufactured at the Philadelphia Mint from 1792 through the early 20th century.

A few years ago Mr. Champa decided to sell his fabulous collection. Bowers and Ruddy Galleries was chosen to sell the coins at combined public auction and mail bid sale. A fine catalogue featuring the Armand Champa Collection and other important consignments was prepared. The preface to this large illustrated volume pointed out the quality of the coins offered:

"Welcome to our combined public auction sale and mail bid sale of the Armand Champa Collection and other important consignments. Whether you attend the sale in person or bid by mail you will receive some truly beautiful coins if your bids are successful.

"Armand Champa, well-known Louisville, Kentucky numismatist, appreciated the finest. His collection, assembled over a period of many years (and including many purchases from us), is replete with many scarcities and rarities. United States pattern coins were a special interest. Mr. Champa's collection, offered here in its entirety, contains many spectacular pieces—including 21 specimens of the famed pattern half dollars of 1877, the rare and beautiful Amazonian silver dollar of 1872, and many other prize coins, many of which trace their pedigrees to the collections of Dr. J. Hewitt Judd, King Farouk, Col. E.H.R. Green, and other prominent numismatists.

"The rare coins in this sale are many. We might mention the gem-condition silver and other coins at the beginning of the catalogue, a consignment which includes some of the most beautiful bust-type quarters we have ever handled. Early Proof coins such as silver three-cent pieces of 1854 and 1857, an 1842 half dime, an 1848 dime, and half dollars of 1847, 1848, and 1857 will surely create interest among specialists. Silver dollars, always a popular series, are highlighted by examples of 1858, 1871-CC, 1873-CC, 1889-CC, 1892-S, 1893-S, and two examples of the famous 1895—not to mention many other beautiful coins.

"If spectacular rarities are your forte you'll have a choice of such pieces as a gem Uncirculated 1876-CC twenty-cent piece (the specimen once owned by noted composer Jerome Kern), an 1879 flowing hair $4 Stella, the ultra-rare (just ten were struck!) 1879 coiled hair Stella, a superb 1803 Proof restrike silver dollar, and many more celebrated coins—many of which have not appeared on the market for years.

"We have enjoyed cataloguing these coins for you. If you are a successful bidder in person or by mail—and we hope that you will be—you'll experience the same enjoyment, but to an even greater degree as it will be combined with the *pleasure of ownership.* Good luck. We hope you can attend the sale in person. If this is not possible, then we'll represent your mail bids. A wonderful sale is now about to take place. Thank you for your participation."

The sale, which occupied two days, was an exciting event. Hundreds of bidders participated by mail and in person. While the excitement, enthusiasm, and action of the Armand Champa Collection sale would make an interesting story in itself, we will mention just one coin here: Lot 1086, a beautiful Amazonian pattern silver dollar which was considered by Mr. Champa to be the highlight of his pattern silver coins. This piece, one of the most beautiful of all American pattern issues, attracted quite a bit of pre-sale attention. Bids by mail and telephone in the amounts of $4,750, $5,000, and $5,300 had been received before the sale. It was the expectation of James Ruddy and me that the piece would be awarded to the $5,300 bidder, a Wisconsin gentleman, at a nominal advance over the second highest bid—perhaps a realization of $5,100 or $5,200.

It didn't work out that way. The coin was sold on the sale floor for $5,500 to a prominent numismatist from Iowa who flew to California to bid on that piece plus a number of others he needed for his collection. Thus a new price record was set!

The sale of this particular coin points out several interesting things; it is a small object lesson in itself. First, Mr. Champa realized a profit of *several thousand dollars* over what he had paid for it a few years earlier. Second, the coin is part of the United States pattern series—a field not considered to be in the mainstream of "hot" issues by many people, thus pointing out that the careful buyer can make tremendous profits by purchasing coins in specialized areas. Third, rarity never goes out of style—and when scarce and rare coins come up for sale new price records are almost always set.

The story of the 1872 pattern Amazonian silver dollar doesn't end there. The underbidder, the Wisconsin gentleman previously mentioned, telephoned me after the sale to see if he had purchased the coin. Naturally he was disappointed to learn that he hadn't. He then asked if we could find another specimen for him. This was a challenge—and James Ruddy and I responded by searching our memories and writing a number of letters to collectors and dealers who might be a possible source. Within a month or two luck was with us, and we obtained not only an 1872 Amazonian pattern silver dollar but the other two Amazonian coins of the same year that were issued with the dollar: the Amazonian quarter and the Amazonian half dollar! This splendid set, an American numismatic classic, is now a prized possession of our Wisconsin numismatist friend.

How well did Mr. Champa do with his investment? This, of course, is Mr. Champa's business and not ours. However, we know he did well for Mr. Champa then did something unprecedented in the annals of American numismatics: he was so pleased with the results of the sale of his collection that he placed advertisements thanking us in leading numismatic publications! The advertisement which appeared in *The Numismatist,* official journal of the American Numismatic Association, is typical:

"Thank you Dave Bowers and Jim Ruddy for the excellent handling of my coins through your American Auction Association. I was well pleased with your wonderful description of my coins, especially the patterns. The prices realized for my coins nearly doubled the offers I received from other dealers. (signed) Armand Champa."

A few months after the sale took place I saw Armand Champa again when he attended the American Numismatic Association convention in New Orleans which that year was held in New Orleans. "Since I have been at the convention here several people have asked me whether or not these advertisements were your idea—and I was happy to tell them that they were completely unsolicited by you," he said with a merry twinkle in his eye! And the statement was absolutely true. The pleasure of helping a discriminating numismatist build a fine collection for investment and pleasure over the years and then later helping him to sell it is one James Ruddy and I have experienced many times. It is a satisfying experience which is difficult to describe in words. Helping others to achieve success is very, very gratifying—and I do not mean gratifying from just a monetary viewpoint.

Answers
to Your
Rare Coin Investment
Questions

Chapter 4
Answers to Your Rare Coin Investment Questions

In the course of advising many collectors and investors over the years James F. Ruddy and I have answered just about every type of question imaginable. In this book it is my intention to answer in a direct and honest way the most significant of these. Some questions have already been answered in preceding chapters, and others will be answered later in the book. And possibly still others will be raised by readers of this volume—and will appear in some future book!

But for the moment here are some questions raised by present-day investors and investors of the past.

Quantity as a Factor

QUESTION: What factor does quantity play in coin investment? Is it better to have a single $5,000 coin, or ten $500 coins, or a large number of 50c coins?

ANSWER: There is no definite right or wrong reply to this. A charting of values over a period of years reveals that great rarities which cost thousands of dollars in the 1950's have soared in value since then—as have pieces which cost just a few dollars at that time. My answer to this question is that it depends upon the amount of money you wish to invest. If you want to invest $100 per month in your collection/investment then it would be foolish to save up your money for two years to own just a single coin, a rarity costing $2,400. Rather, you would undoubtedly experience much more satisfaction of ownership if you were to have a nice portfolio of coins in the $10 to $100 range per item. The inclusion of a few items priced at several hundred dollars would not be out of line.

On the other hand, if you wanted to spend $1,000 per month on your coin investment, then a $2,400 coin might be a logical thing to own—assuming, of course, that it met your other requirements as well.

Coin Price and Marketability

QUESTION: Does the price of a coin affect its marketability?

ANSWER: This is a question which we are often asked. Some buyers are worried that expensive coins might not find ready sale when they are put on the market. This fear is unfounded, and here is the reason why:

The price of a coin is usually based upon the rarity of a coin and the demand for it. As the coin market is an active one, prices have equated themselves with supply and demand. Thus an 1838-O half dollar (to cite one example) is an extremely salable item for there are only a few specimens known to exist of this rarity. In fact, only twenty of these were originally coined!

Of course the number of people desiring 1838-O half dollars is also small—but the number of collectors desiring one, even taking the price into consideration, has always been more than the available supply. So, despite the ups and downs of certain segments of the coin market the 1838-O has always been a "blue chip." Earlier in this book I mentioned 1894-S dimes owned by James F. Ruddy and me over the years. We have also had the pleasure of owning several beautiful 1838-O half dollars. A single specimen will illustrate the price movement of this famous rarity. On April 27, 1962 James F. Ruddy and I purchased for $9,500 the specimen offered by Stack's at the sale of the R.E. Cox, Jr. Collection. We subsequently resold the coin to a prominent eastern numismatist.

1838-O Half Dollar

One of America's classic rarities is the 1838-O half dollar. The specimen illustrated above, from the R.E. Cox, Jr. and the Century Sale auctions, has been purchased and resold by us several times. In many instances famous rarities have become "old friends." When a fine collection is formed—the "Century Collection" being an ideal example—the owner often commissions us to acquire important pieces. Then when the collection is sold years later we often have the chance to handle the coins again. Over the years Q. David Bowers and James F. Ruddy have handled nearly every important United States and world coin rarity.

Only twenty 1838-O half dollars were coined. Of that number, only about half are known today. Several different specimens have passed through our hands during the past two decades.

In 1973 James F. Ruddy and I had the pleasure of putting this coin, a splendid Proof example, on the market again. The price tag? $75,000—a figure which represented a very attractive profit for the collector who owned it.

The 1838-O half dollar has always been a famous American coin. *There has never been a period in American numismatic history in which it was not in demand*—in good economic conditions and in bad. An 1838-O half dollar was worth more in 1970 than it was in 1960. It was worth more in 1960 than it was in 1950. In 1950 it was worth considerably more than it was in 1940 . . . and so on back through numismatic history. Undoubtedly in 1980 and in 1990 it will be worth far more than it is today!

Prime American rarities—the 1838-O half dollar, 1876-CC twenty-cent piece, 1894-S dime, 1804 silver dollar, $4 gold Stellas of 1879 and 1880 are examples—can be perhaps likened to Rembrandt paintings in the art field. They are expensive to be sure, but when a choice one comes on the market it creates a lot of excitement, and usually a new price record is set!

How High Can Coin Prices Go?

QUESTION: How high is high? How far can coin prices go?

ANSWER: The future is unknown, of course, and no one can predict it with accuracy. However on a comparative basis it can be said with certainty that coin prices have a long, long way to go in relation to prices of rarities in certain other fields.

In 1974 we offered an 1804 silver dollar for $200,000. The buyer, who was from Minnesota, subsequently reported a resale at $225,000! The sale of a 1907 MCMVII Extremely High Relief double eagle at $200,000 by Stack's, the sale of an Uncirculated 1794 dollar at $127,500 by Superior Galleries, and the aforementioned (in the first chapter of this book) 1894-S dime offering by us at $100,000 are but a few examples of recent prices for rarities.

When one considers that rare stamps have broken the $100,000 mark on several occasions (one was actually sold for $380,000) and that for a painting to realize a million dollars or more is scarcely news these days, then American coin rarities priced in the $100,000 to $200,000 range seem cheap by comparison! Perhaps for a comparison to end all comparisons we should mention the Velasquez painting *Portrait of Juan de Pareja* which now hangs in New York City's Metropolitan Museum. $5,544,000 was paid for this at an auction sale held by Christie's of London. For the same price one could spend a lifetime collecting United States coins from colonial through territorial gold pieces, and collect them in the finest available condition, and still have money left over! Are coin rarities overpriced? You be the judge!

Rare Coins vs. Common Coins

QUESTION: The average investor will not have the opportunity to own great rarities (such as the 1894-S dime, 1838-O half dollar, etc.). If one cannot own great rarities, then should a collector/investor concentrate on owning just common coins of low value? Or is there a point in between these two extremes?

ANSWER: In answer to this I repeat the old aphorism (old to me; I have said it many times): a common coin that is common today will be common in the foreseeable future. A common coin by very definition is common and is not rare! To buy common coins in the hope that they will magically become rare is a futile effort! This simple admonition is overlooked by many people who buy coins as an investment. This paragraph is so important that I suggest that you underline it in your copy of this book!

Many millions of dollars have been expended by people who prefer quantity to quality. This situation is not unique to coins; it exists in stamps as well. In our sister field of philatelics (stamp collecting) countless misguided souls religiously "invest" in sheets of new postage stamps as they are issued. The sad truth of the matter is that one can purchase from any stamp dealer sheets of stamps that are ten to twenty years old—and pay only face value for them! The investment potential, or lack of it, needs no further explanation. So it goes with hoarding modern coins issued by the zillions.

The best path is to purchase coins which have a present scarcity and value—either realized or unrealized—in the marketplace.

A few years ago I wrote an article for *The Forecaster* in which I recommended the purchase of certain types of United States coins. Taking a Proof Barber half dollar (the random example I mentioned earlier in the book) as an instance, I am happy to note that great profits have been made by anyone who read the *Forecaster* advice and acted on it. Or, for that matter I can point to an even earlier (1963) article which I wrote when Uncirculated Barber halves fetched $20 and Proofs $80, tiny fractions of today's values. Of course this seems like "ancient history." But to be realized is the fact that today will be "ancient history" ten or twenty years from now!

To be desirable for investment a coin does not have to be rare or even extremely scarce. It can be moderately scarce and still do quite well. Scarceness and rarity are relative. As another example take the 1917 Type I Liberty standing quarter issued at the Philadelphia Mint. This particular coin is in great demand for type sets—to illustrate this design (which was made in only two years, 1916 and 1917). The mintage for the 1917 Type I is fairly large: 8,792,000 total. However, 1917 Type I quarters were issued during an era when coin collecting was in its infancy. Few people bothered to save these quarters. Although no figures are known, probably all but a few thousand (at most) went into circulation and became worn as they passed from hand to hand. If we assume that just a few thousand are known today then the pieces are fairly scarce when you consider that there are perhaps several hundred thousand collectors desiring to assemble a type set of 20th century U.S. coins—and that each will need a Liberty standing quarter of the 1916-1917 issue. Even when one considers that many collectors will be satisfied with a coin in a worn grade, the investment possibilities of a 1917 Type I quarter remain obvious. In 1963 we wrote that "the 1917 issue sells well for $22.50 to $25.00 [in Uncirculated grade]. We believe that this price is a strongly-based one and that it will continue to advance." Advance it did, and by 1977 several sales had taken place in the $300 to $400 range!

Let me repeat: to buy common coins in the hope that they will magically become rare is a futile effort. And yet common coins provide the basis for many careless "investment recommendations," simply because common coins are very easy to buy and don't require much effort to locate. On the other hand, scarce and rare coins sell themselves.

Expansion of the Coin Market

QUESTION: What will make the price of coins rise above today's levels?

ANSWER: Of course this is basic economics, but if the number of collectors increases then the demand for rare coins will also increase. Now the question becomes: will the number of collectors increase?

This seems quite likely. The average citizen is working an ever-shorter week. More and more time is being directed toward leisure activities. Coin collecting is an ideal leisure activity. It can be conducted in private, does not require a large amount of space (a fine collection can be assembled by an apartment dweller, for instance), a coin collection can be conveniently and cheaply stored, and so on. As leisure time activities increase, coin collecting will surely increase also. More collectors will bring an even greater demand.

Then there is the international expansion of the market to consider as well. As noted earlier, other countries are developing large numbers of collectors. As the "affluent society" spreads throughout the world there will be more and more attention paid to leisure time pursuits such as coin collecting. This is presently taking place in several countries.

Japanese collectors and dealers are becoming an important factor in the market. England, which had only four major dealers and just a few thousand collectors in the early 1960's (when I used to spend a lot of time there), now has dozens of dealers and tens of thousands of collectors. Germany, Italy, France, and Switzerland have been strong numismatic markets in recent years. Danish, Swedish, and Norwegian collectors have been bidding ever-increasing prices for their own coins as well as for coins of other countries. It makes sense for other buyers around the world to desire American coins—just as American collectors for years have avidly assembled sets of crowns, gold coins, patterns, and other desirable issues of foreign states. Coin collecting, long an international hobby from the viewpoint of the variety of coins collected, is now becoming an international hobby from the viewpoint of collectors collecting them!

Then there is also the important consideration of monetary inflation. If the purchasing power of the American dollar continues to depreciate then the thought of paying $100, $200, or whatever for a coin won't seem to be so important. It wasn't that long ago that $200, for instance, would have been a "big price" for an Uncirculated 1796 quarter. I mention this particular coin for I remember that Aubrey Bebee, the Omaha dealer, showed me a 1796 quarter with a prooflike surface at the American Numismatic Association convention in 1955. He stated that he had paid $200 for it. This was a "staggering price" at the time. Today it seems absurdly cheap. A comparable coin would sell for well over $20,000 on today's market (we sold one at auction for $18,500 in 1974). I don't mean to suggest that the average coin purchased for $200 today will be worth $20,000 in 20 or so years, for I don't think it will be. On the other hand it certainly is reasonable to expect many of today's $200 coins to multiply in value several times.

What Grades of Coins Should I Buy?

QUESTION: What grades of coins should I buy? Is it better to buy, for instance, ten coins in "Good" condition or one coin in "Uncirculated" grade for the same total price?

ANSWER: From an investment viewpoint all grades of coins have done well. Scarce coins in lower grades such as Good and Very Good have been excellent investments over the years, as have been Uncirculated and Proof pieces. However, Uncirculated and Proof coins and other higher grade issues (such as Fine to Very Fine or better for certain 19th century and earlier examples) have been in stronger demand and are scarcer than lower grade pieces, so the dealer's margin of profit is less.

Take as a random example an Uncirculated coin which sells for $50. A dealer might well pay $40 to buy the coin for stock, giving him a profit of 25%. It is the higher grade pieces that turn over the fastest in a dealer's stock, so he is willing to take a smaller margin of profit for them. On some closely-traded high grade items the margin between buying and selling may be only 5% to 10%.

On the other hand if a dealer were to have ten coins in stock, all of the same variety, that were priced at $5 each, he may only want to pay $2 or $3 per coin (for a total of $20 to $30 for the lot) to buy such pieces for stock, as more handling per item is involved. I am assuming that the latter coins are in worn grades. From an investment viewpoint I personally would rather have one Uncirculated $50 coin than ten well-worn $5 coins. There is no strict right or wrong answer to this—it is more a matter of personal preference. It has been said by others that collectors and investors should "buy the best grade they can afford." Generally I agree with this advice.

Accurate Grading is Important

QUESTION: I read a lot about coin grading. Is this an important factor? Do all dealers grade the same?

ANSWER: Grading is very important. Accurate grading is essential. When you purchase coins for investment you are faced with the uncertainty of what they will do in the future.

Will they go up in value or won't they? Of course, we both hope that they will. Why add to this the uncertainty of whether or not your coins are in the correct condition? Instead, be very sure you are buying the grade you expect; the grade you are paying for.

In recent years many coins have been "treated" and "processed." Lower grade coins have been given the false appearance of "Uncirculated" or "Proof." There is a lot of money to be made by selling processed and treated coins. Such operations prey on the bargain seeker.

An Extremely Fine large cent of 1853, a coin worth, say, in the $25 range, if "processed" and wrongly sold as "Uncirculated" for $100 (just a fraction of the going price for true Uncirculated) is no bargain at $100. In fact, you are overpaying by a factor of four or five times! And yet it is continually amazing to see how many collectors, particularly new ones, fall into such a trap. While dealers are sometimes reluctant to discuss "processed" coins, if you want a discussion on this subject you can talk with the representatives of leading numismatic publications. Grading is a big problem. I might mention that ethical dealers do not "process" coins. Your best protection is to buy from an ethical dealer.

Bear in mind also that a large advertising budget has little to do with a dealer's experience or the quality of the coins he sells. Indeed, some of the most successful dealers enjoy a fantastically large business by modestly circulating price lists and auction catalogues to a selected number of proven clients who have been with them over the years. They do not need a continuing stream of new faces! Even worse yet is the so-called "investment advisor" who sells overgraded coins at full retail prices to potential investors—hoping that these collectors will never gain access to other established collectors who might tell them the true condition of their coins. Knowledge of the American Numismatic Association and other organizations is "hidden" from their investors! My reaction to this situation you can easily guess, and there is no sense wasting print on it here.

Do not overlook the grading problem. To this end a copy of the *Photograde* book, written by my associate James F. Ruddy, will pay for itself many times over. This book has been accepted and acclaimed by numismatic publications everywhere as the standard authority in the field of coin grading.

It costs no more, in fact it is infinitely cheaper in the long run (when the time comes to sell your coins), to buy properly graded coins. Otherwise you are just kidding yourself and are impairing the chances for the success of your investment. I do not mean to be negative in a book which perhaps should be 100% positive, but I do want to clarify this situation and make you aware of it. In many years of buying collections I have seen large sums of money lost by collectors who were hoodwinked in this regard. "There is no Santa Claus in numismatics," Lee Hewitt (founder of the *Numismatic Scrapbook Magazine*) has written. This is one of my favorite quotations, so I will mention it here again!

If you are uncertain about coin grading, do some "comparison shopping." The same coin advertised as "Uncirculated" at $100 and $150 can be a better buy at $150 than $100 if, for instance, the $150 is really Uncirculated and the $100 is really Extremely Fine.

The Importance of Authenticity

QUESTION: How concerned should I be with the genuineness of coins offered to me?

ANSWER: Authenticity is important. If you don't know the technical aspects of coin authenticity (and few amateur collectors or investors are expected to know this), then by all means do business with one of the many dealers who guarantees the authenticity of what he sells. Members of The International Association of Professional Numismatists and the Professional Numismatists Guild (to mention the two most prominent worldwide dealers' organizations which are internationally recognized and which have very, very strict admission standards) pledge that their members will

1848 CAL. Quarter Eagle

Made from California gold and specifically identified as such on the coin, the 1848 CAL. $2.50 gold piece is perhaps the most historically significant of all U.S. territorial-related gold coins. Certainly no gold coin bearing the imprimatur of the United States Mint has a closer connection with the famed Gold Rush.

When gold was first discovered at Sutter's Mill in California samples were rushed to the United States Mint for testing and assay. A letter to Dr. R.M. Patterson, Director of the U.S. Mint in Philadelphia, from Secretary of War W.L. Marcy read in part: "If the metal is found to be pure gold, as I doubt not that it will be, I request you to reserve enough of it for two medals ordered by Congress and not yet completed, and the remainder, with the exception of one or two small bars, I wish to have coined and sent with the bars to this department. As many may wish to procure specimens of coin made of California gold, by exchanging other coin for it, I would suggest that it be made into quarter eagles with a distinguishing mark on each."

The distinguishing mark was, of course, "CAL." above the eagle on the reverse. Thus one of America's most romantic and most famous rarities was created. Illustrated above is the superb Uncirculated example which appeared in the Bowers and Ruddy Galleries auction of the Robert Marks Collection.

guarantee the authenticity of coins sold. A refund in full awaits the purchaser of any coin which is later proven to be not genuine. This is a *tremendously important* protection, for a fake coin is absolutely worthless and is, in fact, illegal to own.

Never buy a coin "as is." On the plus side of this situation is that the collector who buys from an established professional dealer is at a great advantage, for only rarely will a professional make an error, and when he does the error will be corrected (as per the International Association of Professional Numismatists and Professional Numismatists Guild requirements mentioned earlier).

However, there are many fake coins for sale elsewhere in the coin marketplace. It should be noted that the number of forgeries in the coin field is less than those in certain other collecting fields. However, unlike the situation in other fields (modern art is an example), publications in our field, that of coin collecting, give great publicity to counterfeiting and the problems it causes. Should this aspect be publicized or shouldn't it be? There are two sides to this question, and we are not sure which side we are on! Our stand on the subject of fakes is well-known: we are against them, and James F. Ruddy and I have spent countless hours working with numismatic associations, government authorities, publications, and others to combat these. We are happy to say that many arrests and convictions have been made as the result of our efforts in this direction! Concerning publicity, however, one camp advocates that fakes should be widely publicized and played up so that everyone takes notice. This undoubtedly scares off many would-be collectors who are afraid to enter the hobby. This emphasis on fakery is NOT a featured part of publications on art, antiques, and so on—although, as noted, the problem exists there to an equal or greater extent than it does in coins. The other camp advocates that fakes be privately handled without fanfare. This second idea would be feasible if all dealers would guarantee their merchandise and collectors could be persuaded to buy only from those dealers. But as no license or even experience is needed to hang up a "Rare Coins for Sale" or "Coin Investment Center" sign, perhaps it is best that fakes be nipped in the bud by publicizing them. This is a controversial point.

I have presented both sides to the authenticity publicity situation—so, rightly or wrongly, you know that this can be a problem. You know also that the problem is a simple one—and that you can do your part. You have no risk whatsoever of a financial loss in this regard if you buy from a dealer member of the International Association of Professional Numismatists or Professional Numismatists Guild (or if the dealer otherwise guarantees IN WRITING that the coins are absolutely and positively genuine).

Aspects of Investment Timing

QUESTION: How long should I hold my coins?

ANSWER: The answer to this depends on your investment objectives. Generally speaking, James F. Ruddy and I recommend a minimum time of three to five years. Really spectacular profits have been shown by our clients who have held their coins from ten to fifteen years, as is often possible with a retirement program or employee benefit fund, for example.

In my personal opinion rare coins should be considered as a long term investment. While short-term profits are possible, by far the largest and most consistent profits have accrued to the long term investor—and I speak from much experience in this regard!

I have seen many fabulous profits made by collectors and investors who assembled fine groupings of coins over a period of years and then sold them upon their retirement. It is not at all unusual for Bowers and Ruddy Galleries to pay $10,000, $25,000, $100,000, or even more for coins which originally cost the customer 1/5th or 1/10th of that sum! I might further add that this is a very, very gratifying aspect of our business. Whenever I look through the many catalogues that James F. Ruddy and I prepared in the 1950's I know that the people who bid in our auctions and ordered from our catalogues back then can be nothing less than delighted if they still have the coins today! The coin market has done wonderfully well for our clients of the past. This in turn has contributed to our own success, for there is no better client than one for whom you've made a lot of money!

Learning About Coins

QUESTION: How can I learn about coins?

ANSWER: When building your coin portfolio—for collecting, for investment, or for a combination of both—it will pay you to learn as much about coins as possible. If you plan to spend a few hundred dollars or more on rare coins then I recommend that you subscribe to several different magazines, join the American Numismatic Association, start a numismatic library, and learn all you can about coins.

There is no substitute for knowledge. Any success I have personally had in the rare coin field I can attribute directly to studying and learning about the coins I have sold. The coin investors who have done the best over the years have been the ones with the most knowledge; the ones who took the time to learn about what they were buying. This point isn't even debatable. In my opinion it is basic.

When you buy coins, compare the prices and quality of several different dealers. Don't compare price alone, for such a comparison is meaningless. Absolutely meaningless. Compare grading and you will see why one "Uncirculated" coin advertised at $100 can be a poor buy and another really Uncirculated piece at $150 can be a great value.

Once you've determined where your best values are from, then take advantage of your new-found knowledge by concentrating your purchases with these dealers who give you the best quality and value for your money. By doing so you will greatly enhance the chances for your investment's success.

Now that I have given you some basic information about

investing in coins I will discuss in following chapters the coins themselves—and different ways to build a meaningful coin investment portfolio; a treasure for the future.

Chapter 5

History

of

United States Coins

The Beginnings of American Coinage

It was not until 1792 that the United States government established its own mint. The need for coins in commerce before then was filled by many different issues from many different sources. Prime in importance were coins issued by major European countries, most importantly England and Spain. It was the usual practice to calculate transactions in terms of English pounds, shillings, and pence or in Spanish dollars and fractional parts thereof.

In addition to the official issues of England, Spain, France, and other countries there were many foreign-made speculative coins which circulated in the early American colonies. William Wood, an English entrepreneur, obtained a royal patent from King George I of England whereby Wood was authorized to privately strike coins for circulation in America (which was an English colony at that time). These coins, bearing the legend *ROSA AMERICANA* ("the American rose"), were issued in the denominations of halfpenny, penny, and twopence. In the 1722-1724 years William Wood also issued a series of coins with a *HIBERNIA* inscription. These pieces, issued in the values of farthing (¼ of a penny) and halfpenny, were not popular with the Irish people for whom they were originally intended, so quantities of them were shipped to America.

Later, in the 1780's and 1790's mainly, a large number of English-made tokens, some of which bore patriotic legends or inscriptions honoring President George Washington, were widely circulated in America. Other tokens and coins with American inscriptions or made with use in the colonies in mind were struck in France, Holland, Spain, and elsewhere.

Among the most interesting of early American or *colonial* (as collectors refer to most pre-1792 issues) pieces are those struck by the colonies themselves, either by state mints or on a contract basis.

Massachusetts produced a distinguished series of silver coins beginning in 1652 and continuing for several decades thereafter. Prominent among these issues are the Pine Tree Shillings; coins which have been mentioned in many romantic tales and stories. "A bent Pine Tree Shilling will ward off witches" was a belief at one time! In 1787 and 1788 Massachusetts produced copper cents and half cents at a state-run mint. The venture was soon abandoned, however, when the state learned that each coin cost twice its face value to produce!

In 1785 the first copper coins of Vermont appeared. Coined by a group of individuals who obtained a contract from the Green Mountain State, the earliest pieces bore a design of an early morning sun peeping over a forested ridge—just the type of scenery one might expect to actually find in Vermont! Later Vermont issues (which were continued through 1788) were changed in appearance to conform more or less to the appearance of British halfpennies of the same era; an effort to make the coins more acceptable in the channels of commerce by giving them a familiar design.

Of all states which issued their own coins Connecticut was by far the most prolific. Over three hundred die varieties of Connecticut cents, which were minted from 1785 to 1788 inclusive, are known today. Most bear the legend *AUCTORI: CONNEC:* ("by the authority of Connecticut"), but interesting blunders and errors occur. One variety reads *CONNECT* instead of *CONNEC*, and others read *AUCIORI, AUCTOPI,* and *AUCTOBI* instead of the standard *AUC-TORI.*

Early Colonial Coins of Massachusetts

"NE" shilling. First made in 1652 the earliest Massachusetts silver shillings are simple planchets with "NE" stamped on one side and "XII" (for 12 pence or one shilling) on the reverse.

Willow Tree shilling. The squiggles and curlicues of this early design have been likened to a willow tree. Made for a limited time, Willow Tree shillings are rare.

An attractive 1652 Oak Tree shilling. Following the original "NE" (for "New England") coinage, Massachusetts silver coins were made with willow, oak, and then pine tree motifs. Most specimens in existence today are of the pine tree style.

1652-dated Pine Tree shilling. Much has been written of these romantic silver pieces in history and fiction.

Left: This Pine Tree shilling, a specimen from the George A. Merriweather Collection auctioned by us in 1973, was once bent. In colonial times a bent coin was said to ward off witches, and many Pine Tree shillings are seen today with evidences of this long-ago practice. Attractive specimens of the Pine Tree shilling can be obtained in the $500 to $1,000 range.

New Jersey issued coins at several different mints. Generally, New Jersey copper coins (dated 1786-1788) are of the same basic motif: a representation of the state insignia with a horse head and plow on the obverse and with a shield on the reverse. New York copper coins were made in many varieties, some of which are major rarities today. Some bear the inscription *NOVA EBORAC,* a latinization of *NEW YORK.*

There were many privately-issued coins circulated in the colonies during the 17th and 18th centuries. Perhaps the most famous of these is the Brasher doubloon, a coin which many numismatists consider to be the most valuable and perhaps the most desirable American issue. Ephraim Brasher, a New York City goldsmith and jeweler, produced this heavy gold coin in 1787, possibly as a pattern or a proposal seeking a coinage contract from the state. The coin, equal in value (about $16 at the time) to the Spanish doubloons of the era, bears certain New York-related inscriptions such as EXCELSIOR (the state motto) and NOVA EBORACA.

Near Granby, Connecticut, John Higley owned a small private copper mine. From his own metal he produced halfpenny-size copper coins dated 1737 and 1739. The first pieces bore the inscription *THE VALUE OF THREEPENCE.* The self-assigned high value of threepence caused the pieces to be rejected. Higley, undaunted, changed the inscriptions to read *VALUE ME AS YOU PLEASE.* J. Chalmers, a goldsmith and silversmith of Annapolis, Maryland, issued silver threepence, sixpence, and shilling pieces dated 1783. Standish Barry, a Baltimore silversmith, produced a silver threepence piece dated July 4, 1790—perhaps indicating that this was a commemorative issue in observation of Independence Day. A few years ago I purchased at a coin convention a beautifully-made silver teaspoon bearing Standish Barry's hallmark. It is still useful today for stirring iced tea (my favorite drink)!

Prior to establishing its own mint in 1792 the government explored several avenues for producing coinage. The 1776

State Copper Coins of the 1785-1788 Era

1785 Vermont copper coin shows the sun peeping over a forested ridge, with a plow below—motifs representative of the Green Mountain State. The reverse reads "STELLA QUARTA DECIMA" — "The 14th star — acknowledging Vermont's status as the 14th state in the Union.

1787 Copper coin of New York.

1787 Connecticut copper coin. Called the "Laughing Head" variety by collectors, the portrait on the obverse bears a silly grin! Many fascinating varieties await the collector of early Connecticut coins.

1785 Connecticut copper coin. The obverse is that of a laureated warrior, a classical design. The reverse bears the Latin legend "INDE ET LIB," an abbreviation for "Independence and Liberty."

1787 Massachusetts copper cent. Coinage of such pieces was abandoned when the state government learned that each coin cost twice face value to produce!

1787 New Jersey copper coin. New Jersey issued coins from 1786 through 1788.

Continental dollar, usually seen in pewter metal (but struck in silver and gold as well), bears a design similar to that found on a variety of Continental currency (paper money) and may have been made under the auspices of the Continental Congress. No official documentation in this regard is known however. Small halfpenny-size copper coins dated 1783 and 1785 bear the legend *NOVA CONSTELLATIO* ("the new constellation") and are said to have been struck in England to the order of Gouverneur Morris, who was assistant financier of the Confederation at one time.

The first coins specifically issued under the authority of the United States government were the Fugio cents of 1787. These pieces portray a sundial on the obverse and have the inscription *FUGIO* ("I fly"—pertaining to the rapid passing of time) and *MIND YOUR BUSINESS*. These were struck on a contract basis by James Jarvis of New Haven, Connecticut, and by others.

The Various United States Mints

In 1792 the United States established its own mint in Philadelphia. During the first year of operation several different pattern and experimental issues were produced. The decimal system was adopted. The dollar became the standard unit, and the one hundred units which made up a dollar were called *cents*. The United States, a relatively new country at the time, emphasized the intrinsic value concept. Legislators agreed that a copper one-cent piece should contain a full cent's worth of copper metal, a silver dollar a full dollar's worth of silver, a gold $5 half eagle a full measure of gold metal, and so on. In 1792 it was realized that for a cent to contain a full value of copper metal it would have to be of very large size—about the size of a present-day half dollar! An interesting solution was proposed by the so-called silver center cent. A tiny plug of silver was inserted in the center of the copper disc or planchet prior to striking it with the dies. This combination of silver (a more valuable metal than copper) and copper sufficed to maintain the metallic value at

Colonial and Early American Coins

The Continental Dollar of 1776 features on the obverse a sundial and two mottos: "Fugio" (I fly — referring to time) and "Mind Your Business." The reverse shows an endless chain of 13 links, each one the name of one of the 13 colonies.

1787 Fugio cent. Issued by a private contractor under authority of the United States government, the Fugio cent is one of the first official coins of our country.

1787 Immunis Columbia cent. Columbia, emblematic of the new American nation, was immune to the world's misfortunes.

1794 Franklin Press token depicts an early wooden hand press.

1723 Rosa Americana twopence. Made in England, this coin was intended for circulation in America (then an English possession). The reverse inscriptions translate to "The American Rose; the Useful with the Sweet."

Coins and Tokens Honoring President George Washington

Only a few specimens are known to exist of the 1792 Washington "Roman Head" cent. The Father of our Country is depicted as a Roman emperor.

1783 Washington & Independence token. Made in England, but intended for sale and use in America—as were many early Washington coins and medals.

1791 Washington cent with small eagle on reverse.

A genuine two-headed coin is this undated (circa 1783) Washington Double Head cent.

"HE IS IN GLORY, THE WORLD IN TEARS" reads the inscription on this sentimental token issued shortly after President Washington's death.

Early United States Coin Issues

The U.S. Mint in 1792.

1792 Half disme

1793 Half cent

Three different types of 1793 one-cent pieces

the desired one-cent figure and permitted the diameter to be smaller. Within a few years the intrinsic value concept for copper coins was abandoned. Much later in American coinage history the intrinsic value concept for silver and gold coins was abandoned also. Today we have a fiat currency; coins and paper money based not upon the intrinsic value of their composition but on the good faith and credit of the United States government.

One of the most interesting pattern issues of 1792 is the half disme. *DISME*, the early spelling of *DIME*, was later simplified by dropping the *S*. Silver bullion for the production of 1,500 pieces is said to have been personally supplied by President Washington. The first public notice of the new Philadelphia Mint's first coinage for circulation, the 1792 half dismes, was mentioned in Washington's fourth annual address on November 6, 1792: "There has been a small beginning in the coinage of half dimes; the want of small coins in circulation calling the first attention to them."

The Philadelphia Mint, which has expanded over the years and which has been in a number of different buildings and locations, remains the largest and most important United States mint today. With the exception of certain nickel five-cent pieces minted from 1942 to 1945 (and which have a "P" on the reverse) Philadelphia-issued coins do not bear a distinctive letter or *mintmark*.

In 1838 three branch mints began the production of coins. The New Orleans Mint issued coins with the mintmark "O"—the previously-mentioned 1838-O half dollar (of which only twenty were coined) being the most famous rarity from this mint. Coinage was conducted at New Orleans from 1838 to 1861 and again from 1879 to 1909. In 1861 the New Orleans Mint was seized by the Confederate States of America. Using earlier U.S.-made dies the Confederacy produced a modest quantity of silver and gold coins during that year. Also produced was the 1861 C.S.A. half dollar with a distinctive reverse design. This coin is a major rarity today.

Also in 1838 mints were opened in Dahlonega, Georgia, and in Charlotte, North Carolina. Coins issued at these mints bear distinctive "D" and "C" mintmarks. Both of these mints were operated only from 1838 to 1861 inclusive, and each produced gold coins.

The Denver Mint, in operation today, commenced producing coins in 1906. Denver-issued coins have a "D" mintmark, similar to that used earlier in Dahlonega. The San Francisco Mint produced its first coins in 1854. Bearing "S" mintmarks, coins were made there until 1955. In the latter year it was announced that the San Francisco Mint was to close its doors—evidently forever. Collectors were delighted when the San Francisco Mint again began producing S-mintmarked coins in 1968. Today Proof coins are made there (in earlier years Proof coins were made at Philadelphia) as are issues for general circulation.

The presence or absence of a tiny mintmark can tremendously affect a coin's value. An 1894 dime in mint condition is worth just 1/1000th of the price of an 1894-S dime, for instance! That tiny "S" mintmark is worth $99,900.00, figuratively speaking, based upon the current valuation of $100,000.00 or more for an 1894-S piece!

Other Aspects of Coinage and Minting

COINAGE METALS: Several different types of metals have been used over the years to make United States coins. Usually the basic metal has been alloyed with other metals in order to impart extra strength or other desirable characteristics. Thus most American silver coins are .900 fine, which means that they are 900 parts silver and 100 parts alloy (mostly copper). Likewise the gold in American gold coins is alloyed with copper to give the otherwise soft metal extra strength.

Copper, nickel, silver, and gold have been the main metals used. However, pattern coins have been produced in other metals; platinum and aluminum, for instance. The zinc-coated steel Lincoln cents of 1943, an issue produced during

World War II when the usual bronze alloy was needed more for war material, represents a unique use of that metal.

The previous intrinsic value concept whereby a silver or copper coin contained full value or nearly full value in metallic content is no longer used for regular United States coinage. Whenever the prices of metals rose so that the metallic content of a coin was greater than its face value the coins would be melted in wholesale quantities. This explains, for instance, why $5 gold pieces of the 1820's and 1830's—coins produced by the tens or hundreds of thousands—are extreme rarities today. Most went to the melting pot. During the 1960's history repeated itself and all U.S. silver coins dated prior to 1965 became worth more than their face value; a situation which led to the melting of untold numbers of pieces.

DENOMINATIONS: Today there are five main denominations of coins produced for circulation: the cent, nickel, dime, quarter, and half dollar. The "silver" dollar piece, first coined again in 1971 after a hiatus since 1935, is more of a souvenir issue than a currency issue.

Since 1792 many different denominations of United States coins have been issued. They are: half cent (1793-1857), cent (1793 to date), two-cent piece (1864-1873), three-cent piece in nickel metal (1865-1889), silver three-cent piece (1851-1873), half dime or silver five-cent piece (1792-1873), nickel five-cent piece (1866 to date), dime (1796 to date), twenty-cent piece (1875-1878), quarter dollar (1796 to date), half dollar (1794 to date), silver dollar (1794 to date), trade dollar (1873-1885), gold dollar (1849-1889), $2.50 gold piece (1796-1929), $3 gold piece (1854-1889), $4 gold piece (1879-1880 pattern issue), $5 gold piece (1795-1929), $10 gold piece (1795-1933), $20 gold piece (1849-1933), and $50 gold piece (1877 pattern issue and 1915 commemorative issue).

Coinage has not been continuous in most instances. As an example, silver dollars were struck bearing the following dates — with large gaps between coinages: 1794-1804, 1836,

1838-1873, 1878-1904, 1921-1928, 1934-1935, and 1971 to date. One-cent pieces have the best record for continuity; they have been struck every year since 1793 with the solitary exception of 1815.

METHODS OF STRIKING: With just a few exceptions coins were meant to be used to fill the need for a circulating medium to aid commerce. Coins struck for circulation are referred to as *business strikes*—which differentiates them from the few pieces struck as Proofs (to which refer) or presentation pieces. Business strikes were produced at the highest speed possible. When mintage was completed the coins would fall into a hopper or bin. From that point they would be put in a bag and shipped into the channels of banking and commerce. An Uncirculated or mint-condition coin is one which has never passed hand-to-hand in circulation. It is typical, however, for an Uncirculated piece to show bagmarks due to the coinage method just described. Sometimes an Uncirculated coin will show one or more tiny lintmarks. Believe it or not, a strand of human hair or a piece of cloth lint (from a wiping rag used to clean a die) is stronger than the coin metal — and such particles are often impressed into a coin's surface.

A coin which possesses only a few bagmarks and is above average Uncirculated may be designated as *Choice*. An especially select piece with a minimum of bagmarks or perhaps with none at all would be graded even higher as *Gem* Uncirculated or, in European catalogues, FDC (for fleur-de-coin). The term *superb* is sometimes used to describe a particularly flawless specimen of a scarcity or rarity, but this is not in popular use. When collecting coins it is important to be realistic in your expectations in this regard. While it is perfectly reasonable to demand and obtain a Choice Uncirculated example of a Washington quarter in the 1930s or 1940s, the finding of a Choice Uncirculated $20 gold piece dated in the 1850s is a virtual impossibility. These large and heavy gold coins were struck for use in commerce, were stored and shipped together in bags, and no thought was given to handling them carefully for future collectors! Seeking to complete a collection of Choice double eagles in the 1850s would only lead to frustration!

The production of coins was not always as efficient or uniform as it is now. Dies were used until they were well worn or until they literally broke apart. In the early days the pressures used in striking and the planchets (metal discs or blanks) were often irregular and inconsistent. As James F. Ruddy has written in his *Photograde* book:

"Variations in variety or striking must be taken into consideration [when grading a coin and comparing it to the *Photograde* photo], especially for coins minted before 1836 and for certain Denver and San Francisco issues in the 'teens and 1920's, for example. The reader must average the plus and minus factors when comparing a coin to the average picture. If any early large cent, for example, shows weak letters on the right, it must be assumed that the coin could not have been worn only on one portion of its surface. Examples such as this result from an improper strike, an uneven planchet, or an improper die alignment. When grading a coin, take into consideration all of the features on each side—not just an isolated weak spot which was not a result of wear."

There is no formula to determine which coin issues are commonly found in sharply-struck condition and which are rarely (or not at all) found that way. Experience is your best guide—your own experience or that of a professional dealer. The 1926-D quarter is an interesting case in point. Nearly all known specimens are flatly struck on the head. In late 1972 an Uncirculated 1926-D quarter catalogued $35.00 in the *Guide Book*, and a choice specimen (relatively free of bagmarks) sold for in the $40.00 range. At the same time Lot No. 1128 of the American Auction Association's sale of the Robert Marks Collection was catalogued thus:

"1926-D quarter. Brilliant Uncirculated. Full head, and of *extreme rarity* as such. The importance of 1926-D, a coin which nearly always is weakly struck, in this sharply struck condition cannot be overemphasized. It would not surprise us at all to see the coin sell for several hundred dollars, and it would be worth it. The final bid is up to you, however." The coin sold for $240.00 to a specialist who recognized its rarity. Today, of course, the coin would be worth far, far more.

When a coin leaves its shipping bag or roll and is placed into circulation it acquires signs of use. Coins in worn grades are classified as About Good (the lowest collectable grade), Good, Very Good, Fine, Very Fine, Extremely Fine, and Almost Uncirculated. I refer you to the *Photograde* book for detailed information on the grading of United States coins in these classifications.

PROOF COINS: Proof coins have a mirrorlike finish and are especially struck for collectors. Due to the extra care involved in striking them, they are sold by the mint for a premium price. Proof dies are carefully made to insure that all details (such as star points, lines in Liberty's hair, etc.) are sharp and distinct. The die surfaces, both obverse and reverse, are polished to a high degree. The coin blanks or planchets are carefully selected to be flaw-free, are cleaned, and then are fed by hand into the coinage press. Sometimes several blows or impressions from the dies are used to bring up the coin design to its full sharpness. The Proof-making process is done at slow speed on special presses using extra striking pressure. When a Proof coin is struck it is removed by hand from the press and carefully set aside to prevent contact with other coins or damaging its surfaces.

Although the Philadelphia Mint produced Proofs in limited numbers from 1817 (the date when suitable equipment for this purpose was first installed) through the 1850's, early Proofs were not generally offered for sale to the public. Rather, they were reserved for dignitaries, visiting foreign officials, and for other presentation purposes.

In 1858 Proof sets were first offered for public sale. In that year 80 silver Proof sets were sold. Contrast that to the 3+ million sets produced on the average each year during the

1960's and early 1970's! From 1858 to 1916 Proof coins were generally available from the mint on this basis: (1) A "minor Proof set" containing copper and nickel denominations from 1c to 5c could be purchased; (2) or a "silver set" containing denominations in that metal from the 3c silverpiece through the silver dollar and/or trade dollar could be bought; (3) or Proof gold coins could be purchased individually. Only rarely would a purchaser buy a full run of Proof coins from the cent through the $20 gold. The Proof mintages for the year 1888 illustrate this: (1) 4,582 minor Proof sets containing the Indian cent, nickel three-cent piece, and Liberty nickel were sold. (2) 832 silver Proof sets containing the dime, quarter, half dollar, and silver dollar were distributed. (3) Individual Proof gold coins were sold as follows: gold dollar 1,079 pieces, $2.50 gold 97 pieces, $3 gold 290 pieces, $5 gold 95 pieces, $10 gold 75 pieces, and $20 gold 105 pieces. The number of pieces in a Proof set of a given year depends upon which denominations were currently being struck for circulation. Contrast the number of pieces in an 1888 set (as just noted) with those in the largest set of all, the 1873. In an 1873 set you will find the following: Indian cent, two-cent piece, nickel three-cent piece, silver three-cent piece, shield-type nickel, half dime, dime without arrows at the date, dime with arrows at the date (the arrows signified a change in the weight of the coin), quarter without arrows, quarter with arrows, half dollar without arrows, half dollar with arrows, silver dollar, trade dollar, and gold coins of the denominations of $1, $2.50, $3, $5, $10, and $20!

Certain Proof coins of the early 20th century are known as Matte Proofs or Sandblast Proofs. These have specially-prepared surfaces with a grainy or matte finish and are entirely unlike the so-called "brilliant" Proofs in appearance. Matte and Sandblast Proofs were coined in the Lincoln cent series from 1909 to 1916, in the Buffalo nickel series from 1913 to 1916, in the $2.50 and $5 gold series from 1908 to 1915, and in the $10 and $20 Saint-Gaudens series from 1907 to 1915. Today Proofs are of the "brilliant" finish.

From 1936 through 1942 inclusive the Philadelphia Mint again issued Proofs for collectors. Sets could be ordered, or individual coins could be bought separately. Proof coinage was suspended after 1942 and was not resumed until sets were offered again in 1950 (at an issue price of $2.10 per set). Proofs were sold by the set only (individual coins could not be ordered) until 1964. In the latter year the critical shortage of coins in circulation, brought about by collectors according to the mint, resulted in a suspension of such "extra" activities as making Proof sets. A few years later in 1968 production was again resumed—this time at the San Francisco Mint. For the first time in history Proof sets were issued with mintmarks on all of the coins.

Token Recalls the Elegance of a Bygone Age

From shortly before the turn of the century until it was destroyed in a spectacular blaze in 1907, San Francisco's famous French-chateau style Cliff House was one of that city's foremost attractions. Built by Adolph Sutro, who earned his fortune in Nevada's Comstock Lode, the Cliff House and the adjacent Sutro Museum exhibited all sorts of interesting things—including a huge "orchestrion," or automatic orchestra operated by paper rolls. When a dime or a dime-size token was put in the slot of this marvelous device, a symphony concert filled the air! The author, a collector of orchestrions as well as tokens pertaining to them, considers this little dime-size "Good for 10c Trade — Drop in Orchestrian" token to be a real prize, although its numismatic value is but a few dollars. This crude (note that "orchestrion" is misspelled as "orchestrian") little token has its own fascinating story to tell—as do thousands of other early coins and tokens. For those with an inquiring mind, such pieces can be wonderful keys to history. A whole book could be written about the Cliff House and Adolph Sutro, for example!

Chapter 6

Building

an

Investment Portfolio

of

U. S. Coins

Different Ways to Invest

There are a number of different ways to invest in United States coins. Which way is "just right" for you depends upon several factors: your objectives, the amount of money you wish to spend, whether you want to emphasize the investment aspect only, whether you want to combine collecting with investment, and so on. There are many opportunities among United States coins. I will discuss each of the different ways. But first let's see how well United States coins as an investment have done during the past quarter century.

Comparison of Coins with Other Investments

How have coins fared in comparison to other investment media? The Bowers and Ruddy Galleries staff did a survey of rare coin prices from 1948 to the present time. We selected at random ten coins representative of the types we have included in our popular Collection Investment Program "portfolios" over the years. We made no attempt to select pieces by hindsight so as to show super-exceptional performance. Rather, we picked pieces which, in our opinion, are truly representative—not "special situations." We charted the price totals at five-year intervals: 1948, 1953, 1958, 1963, 1968, 1973, plus the recent addition of 1977, using the *Guide Book of U.S. Coins* as a pricing reference. Bearing in mind that the cover date of the *Guide Book* is one year ahead of the publication date, we used the 1964 edition to obtain our 1963 prices, the 1969-dated edition to obtain the 1968 prices, and so on.

The group of ten coins used in the study catalogued $130.75 in 1948. By 1977 the value had risen to $8,465.00, an increase of 6374%! By five-year intervals, plus the recent year 1977, the values rose as follows:

1948	$130.75
1953	197.75
1958	406.00
1963	909.50
1968	1,978.50
1973	3,735.50
1977	8,465.00

Stated another way, every $1,000 invested in such a group of coins would have increased to $64,742 twenty nine years later! Note: the coins used in the study were: 1786 Vermont cent, Fine; 1910 Liberty nickel, Uncirculated; 1852 3c silver piece, Uncirculated; 1842 half dime, Uncirculated; 1807 dime, Uncirculated; 1875-S 20c piece, Fine; 1815 half dollar, Uncirculated; 1878-S trade dollar, Uncirculated; 1847 silver dollar, Uncirculated; 1893 Isabella commemorative 25c, Uncirculated.

During the same approximate period the Dow-Jones Industrial average went from 177.30 in 1948 (last day of trading figures used) to about 900 in May 1977 (when this edition was being revised). Actual five-year interval figures are: 1948: 177.30; 1953: 280.90; 1958: 563.75; 1963: 792.95; 1968: 943.75; 1973: 850.86; plus summer 1977: about 920. Stated another way, a $1,000 investment in the Dow-Jones averages, not including re-investment of dividends, would have stood at about $5,189.

At the same time an investment in a savings account at 5% interest (although such interest was not readily available in the U.S.A. in the late 1940s and 1950s), with interest compounded quarterly, would have risen from $1,000 in 1948 to $4,278 by spring 1977.

During the same period inflation caused the purchasing power of the dollar to decline very sharply. According to United States government statistics $1,000 would have declined in purchasing power to less than $400!

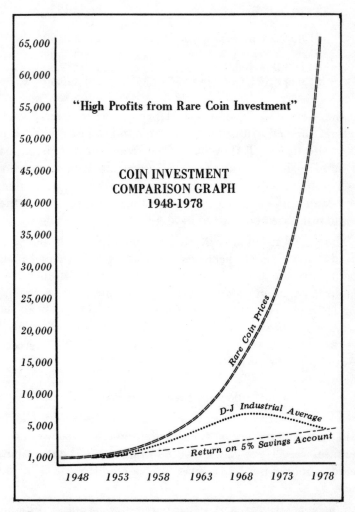

COIN INVESTMENT
COMPARISON GRAPH
1948-1978

"High Profits from Rare Coin Investment"

Rare Coin Prices

D-J Industrial Average

Return on 5% Savings Account

In conjunction with a study prepared for the Bowers and Ruddy Galleries Collection Investment Program I selected at random ten United States coins typical of the types James F. Ruddy and I have been recommending to investors over the years. I made no attempt to select pieces for exceptional performance (which would have been easy to do by hindsight). Rather, I picked coins of the type which you as an investor would have bought on our recommendations 10 or 20 years ago. A list of these coins appears on page 96. As you can see, the comparisons are startling!

In summary, here are the amounts that $1,000.00 would have yielded in these different ways:

Value in 1948	Value in 1977
$1,000 cash purchasing power	400.00
$1,000 5% savings account	4,278.00
$1,000 Dow-Jones	5,189.00
$1,000 RARE COIN INVESTMENT	64,742.00

The preceding figures are rather dramatic, aren't they! Data at the end of this book show a number of different U.S. coins and how well they have done from 1948 to date. Bear in mind again that our selections are random ones, and that even better results could have been listed by simply looking back and finding the very best performers—something that would not have been fair to have done.

The coins listed are of the general types that James F. Ruddy and I have been recommending for years to our clients. In the process our clients have made tremendous amounts of money. We couldn't be happier, for by making our clients successful we have been successful also—and our business has grown steadily to the point at which it is one of the largest and most respected in the world. What greater reward could be asked for?

Our Collection Investment Program

A number of years ago word of the success of our clients' coin investments began to spread. Soon we received such inquiries as: "How can I invest in rare coins?" and "I have heard about your customers' successes. How can I join them?"

James F. Ruddy and I began our *Collection Investment Program,* a plan whereby the investor could buy from us *choice rare coins:* coins of proven scarcity and value. We delivered to our clients coins which we hoped would be of even greater value to collectors in the future: top-grade Uncirculated and Proof coins of the past century and selected

Fine or better earlier issues. The Collection Investment Program was offered as follows in our catalogues:

Our Collection Investment Programs offer a number of advantages. You enjoy the prestige and satisfaction of doing business with one of the world's largest and most respected numismatic firms; a firm which has handled millions of dollars worth of coins, including nearly every major rarity in the book; a firm of unquestioned financial reputation and integrity.

By means of our Collection Investment Programs you can build an IMPORTANT and MEANINGFUL group of rare coins simply by making payments at your convenience. Over the years our clients have found coins to be a wonderful hedge against inflation. Coins represent an outstanding investment with excellent potential for future appreciation. Our Collection Investment Programs make it easy for you to assemble a group of really CHOICE and HIGH-QUALITY coins.

There are no service charges of any kind to pay. You pay just our regular competitive market price for coins—sometimes even less (in the instances of quantity purchases when we pass a special buy on to you), but NEVER more! There are no postage and handling charges, no advisory fees, no "extras" of any kind.

YOU ARE UNDER NO OBLIGATION. You are not signing any tricky contract. If you are not 100% delighted with the coins you receive in our Collection Investment Program you can cancel without notice at any time simply by discontinuing your payments. There is no obligation of any kind to continue. This puts us in the spotlight—we have your "command performance" to provide the QUALITY and VALUE you demand.

FIRST CHOICE: When you participate in our Collection Investment Program you have first pick of one of the largest and finest stocks of selected choice and rare United States and world coins in existence. As new collections and other purchases are constantly being added to our inventory you'll get first pick of many of the most desirable pieces.

YOU DO BUSINESS WITH AN ESTABLISHED FIRM. James F. Ruddy and Don Suter (Manager of our Investment Department) personally supervise the program and the selection of coins you will receive, with the assistance of Q. David Bowers and others. (Unlike many other firms, we don't have "salesmen" as our managers, we have professional numismatists of international reputation.)

Advantages for Us

The Collection Investment Program has two main advantages for us. In a way they are advantages for you, too! They are:

(1) We are able to place directly many beautiful coins without the expense of "sold out" letters, credit problems, advertising preparation and listing, and so on—resulting in a savings for us. In a high-volume, low-margin-of-profit business this savings can be quite important.

(2) Our main problem is BUYING coins, not selling them! By placing with selected buyers such as yourself these choice coins we hope to have the opportunity to buy them back someday. There is no obligation for you to sell your coins back to us. You can sell them wherever you please—as the marketplace is free and competitive. However, it has been our happy experience that many, many collectors and investors who purchased coins from us back in the 1950's and 1960's have kept us in mind—and we have bought their holdings when they were later re-offered to us. Without exception, to our knowledge, each seller has realized a substantial profit! So, by selling you CHOICE COINS OF HIGH QUALITY today we hope you'll keep us in mind in the future, and that you'll help us with our purchase requirements five, ten, or fifteen years from now!

How Our Collection Investment Program Works

Each month (or other interval you choose) we will sell you a group of choice high-quality coins. These pieces will be coins with established numismatic values (as opposed to recent speculative issues). Coins will be in HIGHER GRADES: Uncirculated or Proof, or in the instance of certain rarities or very early pieces, in Fine or better condition.

If you are interested in short-term speculation, this program is NOT for you, and we respectfully recommend that you buy elsewhere. There are countless "investment advisors" in the field of modern speculative issues, and we're not among them. We are ESTABLISHED PROFESSIONAL NUMISMATISTS with a proud heritage to protect—and we are not about to change our style! You'll receive CHOICE COINS OF PROVEN VALUE.

These coins will be like those which have paced the market in the past: scarce gold coins, Uncirculated silver dollars, choice U.S. type coins (coins needed for inclusion in type sets), key dates, and similar items. Circulated modern coins of the type that are not rare now, nor will they be in the foreseeable future, will NOT be included! Rather, you will receive the "blue chips" of numismatics.

Each month (or interval) you send us $100, $250, $500, $1,000, or more. We will then send you choice, selected coins. Each coin will be graded carefully and will be priced and invoiced individually, so you can maintain a record of your purchases (and we will keep a record here also).

GUARANTEE: Here is what we guarantee: We guarantee that you will find our grading to be accurate and the price paid to be reasonable. After receiving your coins you have seven full days to consider the coins, examine them, have them appraised by others, and to consider them in any other way that you wish. If, for any reason whatsoever, you are not 100% delighted, your money will be refunded in full as per our guarantee. There is no red tape. In fact, no explanation is necessary!

GUARANTEED AUTHENTICITY: Each and every coin sold to you by Bowers and Ruddy Galleries is absolutely guaranteed authentic. Over the years we have acted as consultants to government agencies, numismatic publications, and others in matters involving authenticity. You can be sure when you buy from Bowers and Ruddy Galleries, Inc.

––––––––––

So ends the basic description used for our Collection Investment Program. It typifies, in my opinion, how an intelligent investment in rare coins can be made by a successful businessman or professional person in combination with a leading professional numismatic firm.

Building a "Portfolio" of Rare Coins

In working with pension plans, profit-sharing programs, and many individual investors over the years James F. Ruddy, Don Suter, our staff, and I have learned that there are many buyers who do not want to become serious numismatists. On the other hand, they do want to take advantage of the possibilities offered by rare coin investment.

We have developed some guidelines for our own use here at Bowers and Ruddy Galleries. As you will see, the precepts are set up to benefit the investor and to give him what we consider the best chance possible for the success of his investment. While many factors enter into the selecting of coins for an investor, and while sometimes our ideas are modified by an investor's personal preferences, we have found these basic guidelines are of great assistance when we build a "portfolio" of rare coins for a client. I might mention here that these guidelines are NOT the most profitable for our firm, for the margins of profit on high quality coins are not what they are on circulated pieces. However, as stated earlier, we are thinking of the long term—and years from now many of the coins we sell today will come back to us for inclusion in our auction sales and other catalogues. We are now in the 1970's reaping the benefits of the seeds we sowed back in the 1950's and 1960's when we gave what we considered to be good advice to our clients.

"Portfolio" Guidelines for Success

Here are the points which I consider essential for successful building of a "portfolio" of rare coins for investment:

(1) GRADE: I recommend that all coins dated within the past one hundred years be in Choice Uncirculated or Proof grade. There should be no particular preference, in my opinion, between one grade or the other. That is, there is no reason why a group of coins should be limited to either all Uncirculated pieces or all Proof pieces. Proof is a *different* grade from Uncirculated, not a superior grade. In many instances Uncirculated pieces are far rarer than Proofs, for Proofs were specifically saved by collectors whereas Uncirculated pieces weren't. Of course, Denver, pre-1968 San Francisco, New Orleans, and other mintmark varieties are normally not available in Proof grade.

Coins more than a hundred years old are quite acceptable in lower grades: Fine to Extremely Fine, for example. I do not recommend purchasing coins in less than Fine grade. Grades such as Fine, Very Fine, and Extremely Fine represent a happy compromise between quality and price among many early (more than one hundred years old) issues.

(2) QUALITY: I recommend that you purchase *choice* examples of each grade desired. Uncirculated and Proof pieces should be of choice quality. Earlier (more than one hundred years old) pieces in Fine to Extremely Fine should be free of unusual marks or defects.

Avoid like the plague any coin which has been "treated" by buffing or "whizzing." Coins should have natural surfaces: either brilliant or attractively toned.

Remember that one of the main ways that certain "investment advisors," including some with beautiful brochures and expensive advertisements in financial publications, make money is by selling overgraded coins. This point has been mentioned several times in this book, and it is worth mentioning again—simply because it is so important. A certain coin may be worth the following prices: Fine $20, Very Fine $30, Extremely Fine $50, AU (nearly Uncirculated) $100, Uncirculated $200, Choice Uncirculated $250. If someone sends you an AU coin worth $100 and calls it either "Uncirculated" or "Choice Uncirculated" and charges you $200 or $250 (or even a "bargain" $150), then you've been stuck—pure and simple. Don't be lulled by cleverly-worded guarantees promising this and that. Remember: a coin is either of high quality or it isn't. A poor-quality coin will always be worth less than a high-quality one, and a poor-quality coin surrounded by all sorts of fancy words, guarantees, etc. only means that not only is it of poor quality, but that chances are you really paid a lot to get it!

So, the concept of quality is not only necessary, it is *vital.*

(3) DIVERSIFICATION: If you are building a general group of coins for investment, and if collecting interest is not a factor, then there is no reason why you should not acquire a number of duplicates of various issues, providing that the pieces seem to have merit. I do recommend, however, that you acquire duplicate pieces only after you have diversified your holdings.

While the specialized collector will do fine in a certain area—whether it be half dimes, colonial coins of Connecticut, or Proof $20 gold pieces—this is not for the general investor. As an investor you will want to spread your investment over a number of different series. The reason for this is simple: no area of U.S. coins ever moves upward steadily. Rather, the movement is a series of spurts of activity, then a period of lessened activity, and then another leap forward. By averaging your investment among different denominations and types of coins you spread your risk and lessen the speculative element.

(4) RARITY: Unless you are a commodities expert or specialist (in which event you might be interested in bulk

bags and quantities of coins), I recommend purchasing coins of proven scarcity and rarity. As I mentioned earlier, coins which are common today will be common tomorrow. A common coin cannot magically become rare! Also to be remembered is the fact that a dealer's handling is usually the same on a $5 coin as on a $50 coin, so if you buy ten $5 coins rather than one $50 coin you pay ten times more for the dealer's efforts! For the investor who wishes to spend from $100 to $250 per month I generally recommend individual scarce or rare coins with values in the $25 to $250 range, with an occasional higher or lower priced coin if it has exceptional merit. If you want to spend more per month, if you want to invest a lump sum of several thousand dollars or more, or if you are a major investor (such as a profit-sharing or pension fund), then the field of major rarities offers many exciting possibilities. The 1894-S dime mentioned at the beginning of this book—a coin which I bought for $4,750 in 1957 and which is worth more than twenty times that now, is an example. All of the classic American rarities have made great profits for their past owners. Added to this is the prestige of owning the "rarest of the rare" and the fact that rarities always add a dimension of prestige, distinction, and often extra value to a group of coins when they are offered for sale, particularly at auction.

(5) INFORMATION: I recommend that you keep in touch with the coin market, even if you don't anticipate becoming a serious numismatist but are buying coins mainly for investment. Participants in Bowers and Ruddy Galleries' various programs, including the highly successful Collection Investment Program, keep abreast of happenings in the numismatic field by receiving our own *Rare Coin Review*, the sale catalogues issued by our American Auction Association division, our *Special Coin Letter* newsletter, and other offerings. In addition, I recommend that you subscribe to at least one or two numismatic periodicals and join, if you will, the American Numismatic Association. You'll then receive a lot of coin literature in your mailbox. Some of it you can

read casually, others carefully—but at least you'll keep abreast of current trends and ideas.

In addition to the preceding guidelines you need a close relationship with one or more rare coin firms. It is important to remember that there is no substitute for professional experience, and your friendship with a leading dealer can repay itself many times over. Compare quality, value, service, and expertise and do business with the one(s) that treat you the best.

Large-Scale Investing

For the profit-sharing program or pension fund rare coins offer an attractive investment. Over the years James F. Ruddy and I have worked with many accounting firms, banks, financial institutions, and professional planners in this field. Often the initial inquiry came about something like this:

"Our fund participants keep reading about the coin market and its investment potential. Right now we are mainly invested in stocks, bonds, cash, and real estate. I think our people would find coins to be interesting also."

Once a fund or plan adds coins, the chances are excellent that the interest will deepen. We help this in a way by making available to the fund's participants our catalogues and other literature so the people involved have a real sense of participation. Coins and money are a popular subject with everyone!

Coins can be logically classified by date, mintmark, and grade. Values are easily obtainable. Coins can be safely stored in a small space. All of these advantages, plus the others mentioned earlier contribute to coins being the ideal way a pension fund or profit-sharing plan can invest in this area. And, the past performance of coins will stand close comparison to *any* other investment medium.

Selling Your Coins

"What about liquidity? Are coins easy to sell?" This question is a logical one to ask. Coins are indeed easy to sell. It would be difficult to think of any other type of collectors' item which has a more active market.

Choice coins (and these are the type I recommend, as per my comments a few paragraphs earlier) have always been in demand. In the twenty years James F. Ruddy and I have been in the coin business there has never been even a slight slackening of demand for choice and rare coins—and this includes periods of international uncertainty, stock market plunges, political problems, etc. If anything, such uncertainties *increase* the demand for "hard" items such as rare coins!

As dealers we know that our main problem has been buying coins, not selling them. In eager competition dealers will vie to obtain your material. Never, repeat never, have I ever heard of anyone having the slightest difficulty selling a group of choice and rare coins of the types I recommend that you buy.

There are several ways to sell. Here are some of them:

(1) You can have one or several dealers submit offers for your coins—and then take the highest offer.

(2) You can consign your coins to a dealer who can then sell them over a period of time to his customers, to other dealers linked with him by an inter-dealer Teletype system, and to other customers.

(3) You can consign them to be sold at public auction sale.

Of the three main ways, I generally recommend selling by auction. There are several reasons for this. First, if you have been following my advice and have been buying *choice* and *selected* pieces, then you have the real "blue chips" of the coin field. Such coins have traditionally brought the highest prices in auction sales conducted over the years by Bowers and Ruddy Galleries, Inc. If you have major rarities, then I particularly recommend sale by auction. The Matt Rothert Collection sale is a case in point:

In November, 1973 the Auction Department of Bowers and Ruddy Galleries offered for sale the magnificent collection formed over a long period of years by Mr. Matt Rothert, distinguished past president of the American Numismatic Association. Up for bidding were many extremely rare, finest known, and desirable items in all categories—all in all, one of the finest collections ever to come on the market. The report of the sale results noted:

"The emphasis was on *quality*. Quality was the 'buyword' at the Matt Rothert Collection sale. Perhaps this is most poignantly demonstrated by stating that all of the major rarities, without exception, sold for record-breaking prices . . ."

Later on in the report was another interesting paragraph, which I mention here as it re-iterates the "philosophy" of this book:

"One buyer, who was attending his first auction sale, remarked that 'It is obvious that it is quality that sells. It seems that nearly everything choice and rare is bringing well over catalogue prices. It is amazing that there is so much interest considering that the Dow-Jones stock averages have dropped over 100 points in the past few weeks [this was in November, 1973], the Mid-East situation is still unresolved, and our country has so many political and financial problems.' What our friend will soon learn is that coins and coin prices transcend all political and geographical barriers, and in times of uncertainty such 'hard money' items often are the best investment of all!"

Selling at auction removes the uncertainty of the "did I sell my coins for the right price?" question. The research, price calculations, estimates, etc. are done by others. All you do is consign your coins and pay a modest commission on the sale results.

"How soon can I get cash for my coins?" is often another question asked. Well, if you sell your coins directly to a dealer then you get instant cash. You don't even have to wait seven days or so (as is the case with most securities investments). Bowers and Ruddy Galleries pays "cash on the barrelhead" for the coins it buys—simply because the market is so competitive that if we didn't want to pay for the coins right away, someone else would!

Auction also offers fast payment. If you consign your coins for sale, then you will be paid on the settlement date after the sale takes place. The total time from consigning your coins to the time you get your money is several months—usually less time, in fact, than it takes to put (for example) a piece of real estate on the market, sell it, and complete all of the "paperwork." If immediate cash is a necessity then a cash advance can be made against the final auction proceeds.

In practice, the situation of liquidity and ease of sale has never been a problem for any of our clients who have purchased choice and rare coins, but as the question is sometimes asked at the beginning, I give my comments on it.

Summary

For the investor coins offer what I consider to be the ideal investment. Past performance has been spectacular, and with continuing inflation, world monetary problems, the recurring uncertainties of certain other investment fields, etc., coins offer an attractive alternative. James F. Ruddy, Don Suter, and I have personally helped many of our clients make fortunes by investing in coins.

You need not be a numismatic scholar or dedicated collector to invest successfully. It is necessary, however, to follow some common-sense rules (the ones I proposed are recommended!) when you spend your money—and to enlist the assistance of a *professional numismatic firm with an established and unquestioned professional and financial reputation* (in contrast to someone who is mainly interested in taking your money and selling things to you as fast as possible, with the hope that you won't "discover" other dealers, the American Numismatic Association, and so on!).

Do these things, and chances are excellent that your investment will do very well for you. In addition you'll find that your investment is *interesting* to you, your family, and your business associates (if you choose to share your knowledge with them) — for coins and money are something they can relate to; something of interest to everyone.

When time comes to sell your coins you have several methods to choose from. The coin market is competitive, and the type of coins you have will always bring the best prices.

In this chapter I have discussed how you can build a worthwhile "portfolio" of rare coins and have given you the guidelines that have meant great success for our clients in the past. There are, however, many other ways to invest in coins, particularly if you want to combine your investment with an interest in collecting as well. Also, there are several types of specialized numismatic investments. The following chapters will tell some of the other ways which can be quite profitable.

Chapter 7

U. S. Type Set Investment

A Treasure for the Future

In the preceding chapter I gave you my thoughts concerning coin investment in general. The guidelines for quality, keeping aware of the coin market, and so on as given in that chapter are relevant for this chapter also. The preceding chapter discussed how to go about building a general "portfolio" with the assistance of a rare coin dealer to help you. In the present chapter I tell of some different ways to invest. The advantages of building a type set are discussed, and then in the following chapter I review specialized collections. Either way—collecting by types or by specialized varieties—it is possible to combine numismatic enjoyment with a worthwhile investment.

In this regard the life of Oscar G. Schilke comes to mind. Mr. Schilke, who passed away several years ago, was a firm friend and advisor for many years.

I first met Oscar at one of the early Metropolitan New York coin conventions in 1954 or 1955. He had read some of my advertisements in *The Numismatic Scrapbook Magazine* and *The Numismatist* and had some coins to offer for sale. If memory serves, they were a few large cents and colonial coins—two or three hundred dollars' worth in all. Oscar never put a price on anything, so I made an offer—which was accepted.

At the time I attended most of the major conventions in the eastern United States. Oscar was a habitual convention-attender, and at most shows he would have five or six or perhaps even a dozen coins for me to see first. He knew that I liked unusual coins, so he would nonchalantly include a surprise in each selection. As I looked through the envelopes he would wait until I came across the Special Coin and commented on it. On one occasion it was a blazing mint-red Uncirculated 1823 large cent, another time it was a large cent with a small counterstamp commemorating the return visit of Lafayette to the United States in 1824, and still another time it was an 1859 Proof U.S. silver dollar with the perfectly counterstamped impression on obverse and reverse of the Proof dies of the tiny 1859 half dime—literally two coins in one!

In time Mr. and Mrs. Schilke and I became good personal friends in addition to our business acquaintance. Soon I considered a yearly visit to his tranquil lakeside home in Connecticut to be a "must" on my calendar. During these visits Oscar would tell stories of the "good old days" and the experiences he had with collectors and dealers in the 1930's and 1940's.

Many of Oscar's stories remain in my mind. One that's particularly vivid concerns his purchases from one of New York City's dealers. This dealer, Wayte Raymond, who is now deceased, would ask Oscar a certain price for a desired coin and then grant a discount if Oscar could tell him, before buying it, of the coin's background and history!

As did many collectors of the past, Oscar really enjoyed his coins. To aid in appreciating what he purchased and also to learn about coins in general, he built up a large numismatic library—much of which simply "grew" as he saved periodicals, auction catalogues, and other references.

During the late 1950's and early 1960's James F. Ruddy and I purchased many of his coins and sets. Oscar would delight in telling me that "I paid $5 for that one in 1938" as he accepted my offer of $50 for a coin!

Numismatics made Oscar Schilke's life richer in many ways. From a pleasure viewpoint he really enjoyed the company of other collectors and dealers, many of whom can recall today his warm hospitality and his love for the coins he owned. From a financial viewpoint his coin collection made a nice nest egg—an investment whose performance would have been hard to duplicate in any financial medium. Oscar was a businessman himself, and over a period of years he tried many investment areas. Finally he decided—and this was in an era when few people had ever heard of coin invest-ment—that the best investment of all was to spend money on his coin collection. His interests knew no limits, and he formed fine collections of U.S. one-cent pieces, colonial coins, quarter eagles, colonial and U.S. paper money, California gold, and other series.

Coins were very good to Oscar. His life story is an interesting case in point: coins can be a *wonderful investment* in combination with a *fascinating hobby*. Literally, you get the best of two worlds!

To paraphrase Ben Franklin: "Mind your collection carefully, and the investment will take care of itself." By carefully collecting choice coins you'll build a financial treasure for the future. In the meantime you'll have lots of enjoyment in the search for the pieces you need!

There are many ways to build a collection of coins. In the following pages I discuss the advantages of some of the most successful ways.

INVESTING IN U.S. COINS BY DESIGN TYPES

One of the most popular and historically one of the most successful ways to collect and invest in United States coins is by building a type set. Type sets can take several forms—from a representative grouping of 20th century coins to a complete type set which would include one of each major design regularly issued from 1793 to date.

Years ago it was possible to build a virtually complete collection of United States coins by dates and mintmarks. Today it is virtually impossible to do this. First of all, the existing fixed supply of scarce and rare issues has been widely dispersed among hundreds of thousands, if not millions, of collectors. Second, the cost of a nearly complete collection of each and every variety of United States coin ever issued would be prohibitive. A practical alternative is the type set.

A complete type set of United States coins is of immense historical interest. Each design has its own story to tell. Such a set provides an excellent opportunity to learn about the design, history, and romance of each coin. At the same time a type set can be an excellent investment. Years ago James F. Ruddy and I always recommended a type set of United States coins as the ideal way to begin a collection-investment of rare coins. Our many clients who followed our earlier advice have profited spectacularly in the intervening years. It seems assured that collecting by design types will be even more popular in the future. With increasing popularity, price increases are bound to come.

The price of a type set depends on the condition of the coins. This is illustrated by considering the price of a 1793 half cent, for example. The value of this coin as listed in the 1977 edition of the *Guide Book of U.S. Coins* is: Fair $200, Good $415, Very Good $575, Fine $975, and Very Fine $1,700. Very Fine was the best grade listed, simply because specimens are rarely seen in higher grades of preservation. An Uncirculated piece, if indeed one could be found, would be valued in the $10,000 to $20,000 range.

It is therefore important to establish a goal as to the condition desired. Unless you had in mind spending several hundred thousand dollars it would be impractical to aspire to form a complete type set of Uncirculated and Proof grades (Proofs of many issues are available after 1858). As a matter of practical consideration I recommend that issues from 1793 through about 1850 be collected in Fine to Very Fine or Extremely Fine grades. Designs from 1850 to date can be collected in Uncirculated or Proof condition.

Another possibility is to collect issues from 1793 to 1850 in Fine or better condition, from 1840 to the 1890's in Extremely Fine or better condition, and all 20th century issues in Uncirculated and Proof grades. There is no rule about this, and historically all conditions have advanced in value. The selecting of grades desired is dependent upon your personal financial considerations. I recommend buying the best grade you can afford.

In a complete set of United States coins by design types there are a number of rarities. The 1793 half cent mentioned earlier is one of these. This issue is desirable for several reasons: (1) It is essential for a type set, for 1793 was the only year in which the design with the Liberty head facing left and a cap on the pole was used. In the following year, 1794, the design was changed. (2) It is the first United States half cent (half cents were minted from 1793 to 1857). (3) It is one of just two denominations (the cent is the other) struck for circulation in the first full year of the Philadelphia Mint's operation. (4) The coin is rare in its own right. Only 35,334 were minted. Using the *Guide Book* as a reference a 1793 half cent in Fine grade was valued at $50 in 1948. Twenty nine years later in 1977 the same coin catalogued for $975. You can see that a piece held for this span would have yielded a profit of over 1,800%. Further, if the price movement of the 1793 half cent is charted by five-year intervals there was no period in which a profit was not shown from the earlier five-year time. The same is true, by the way, for nearly all U.S. type coins. In fact, the performance of the 1793 half cent is exceedingly *conservative* in comparison to many other issues. For example, an 1862 Uncirculated half dime (representative of the 1860-1873 design type) sold for $1.25 in 1948 and $225.00 in 1977—for a gain of 17,900%!

Another major rarity is the 1796 quarter, a design issued only in that year. A Fine specimen catalogued $70 in 1948. By 1977 the catalogue value had advanced to $3,000. Very rare also is the half dollar design of 1796-1797. A Fine specimen of a 1797 half dollar was valued at $225 in 1948 and $6,000 in 1977.

Among United States gold coins the scarcest major design type is the quarter eagle ($2.50 gold piece) of 1808. In Fine grade this coin was valued at $150 in 1948. By 1977, 29 years later, the piece had advanced to $4,250. In Uncirculated grade the progress of the 1808 was even more dramatic: from $250 in 1948 to $25,000 in 1977!

When building your type set select one of the more common issues within the design range. For example, Liberty walking half dollars were first minted in 1916 and last minted in 1947. Within this span there are dozens of different date and mintmark varieties. In Uncirculated condition 1921 and 1921-D (Denver Mint) each sell in the $2,000 range. Many other scarce and rare issues bring in the $100 to $1,000 range. Rather than select one of these rarities for your type set, select one of the so-called "common" dates in the 1940's. A very choice Uncirculated specimen is currently available in the $20 to $30 range.

There are several ways to build a type set:

The Twentieth Century Type Set

A type set of 20th century United States coin designs makes a very beautiful display. In Choice Uncirculated condition a set is currently valued in the $2,000 range. In my opinion such a set, a set which has been a really excellent investment in the past, will continue to be a great investment in years to come. The set is a nice steppingstone to a larger type set if you later decide to expand your collection to include earlier issues.

Such a collection would include a choice Uncirculated example of each of the following major 20th century coin designs: (1) Indian cent, (2) 1909 V.D.B. cent, (3) 1909-1958 type cent, (4) 1943 steel cent, (5) 1944-1945 shell case cent, (6) Lincoln Memorial cent, (7) Liberty nickel, (8) Type I 1913 buffalo or Indian nickel, (9) Type II

Coin Designs of Our Own Time

Above is a montage of the obverses of the thirty three different coin designs (and different metal types) needed to form a complete type set of 20th century United States coins from the cent to the silver dollar.

1913-1938 buffalo or Indian nickel, (10) 1938 to date Jefferson nickel, (11) 1942-1945 "wartime" nickel, (12) Barber dime, (13) 1916-1945 Mercury dime, (14) 1946-1964 Roosevelt dime, (15) 1965 to date clad dime, (16) Barber quarter, (17) 1917 type I Liberty standing quarter, (18) 1917-1930 type II Liberty standing quarter, (19) 1932-1964 Washington quarter, (20) 1965 to date clad Washington quarter, (21) 1776-1976 bicentennial quarter in silver, (22) 1776-1976 bicentennial quarter in clad metal, (23) Barber half dollar, (24) Liberty walking half dollar, (25) Franklin half dollar, (26) 1964 Kennedy silver half dollar, (27) 1965 to date Kennedy half dollar in clad metal, (28) 1776-1976 bicentennial half dollar in silver, (29) 1776-1976 bicentennial half dollar in clad metal, (30) Morgan silver dollar, (31) Peace silver dollar, (32) Eisenhower dollar in silver metal, (33) Eisenhower dollar in clad metal, (34) 1776-1976 Eisenhower bicentennial dollar in silver metal, (35) 1776-1976 Eisenhower bicentennial dollar in clad metal.

If you want to begin a collection, I recommend that you build a 20th century type set. If your budget permits, then I recommend a complete type set of U.S. copper, nickel, and silver coins. Your 20th century type set is an integral part of a complete 1793 to date set, and is an ideal beginning.

Complete Type Set of U.S. Coins

A complete type set of United States coin designs from 1793 to date is a beautiful collection to behold. As mentioned earlier, such a set has been a wonderful investment in the past. As collecting coins by types is growing in popularity, it seems certain that these will be excellent investments in the future as well.

There are several ways to formulate what a complete type set of United States copper, nickel, and silver coins should contain. The number of pieces depends upon whether or not certain early issues are considered to be "types" or simply varieties of major types. You can leaf through the pages of the *Guide Book of U.S. Coins* and come up with your own ideas.

Generally, a type set should contain one specimen of each major design of each denomination from the half cent through the silver dollar, and covering the span from 1793 to date. On page 203 I list what I consider to be the major varieties. There are several excellent album-type holders as well as display-type plastic holders on the market. You may want to acquire a set of Whitman "Bookshelf" albums or the Coin and Currency Institute's "Library of Coins" albums (to mention just two popular brands; there are others as well) before you begin, and use the openings in the album to determine which pieces you will collect. The "Capital" brand plastic holders make a nice way to display your type set when it is completed. For relatively little expense the "Capital" holders can be custom made to suit your requirements.

Your complete type set of coins will contain from one to over a dozen each of the following denominations: half cent (issued from 1793 to 1857), cent (1793 to date), two-cent piece (1864-1873), silver three-cent piece (1851-1873), nickel three-cent piece (1865-1889), nickel five-cent piece (1866 to date), half dime (1794-1873), dime (1796 to date), twenty-cent piece (1875-1878), quarter dollar (1796 to date), half dollar (1794 to date), silver dollar (1794 to date), and trade dollar (1873-1885).

Some denominations will be represented by only a single coin in your type set. For example, all of the twenty-cent pieces issued from 1875 through 1878 are of the same design, so you will need only one piece. The same is true of the two-cent piece (1864-1873), nickel three-cent piece (1865-1889), and the trade dollar (1873-1885).

Other denominations offer a wide variety of types. In the half dollar series, for example, there are the following designs: (1) Flowing hair type of 1794-1795; (2) Draped bust, small eagle type of 1796-1797; (3) Heraldic eagle reverse type of 1801-1807; (4) Capped bust type with lettered edge, 1807-1836; (5) Small bust type with reeded edge, "50 CENTS" on reverse, 1836-1837; (6) Small bust type with reeded edge, "HALF DOL." on reverse, 1838-1839; (7) Liberty seated type without motto, 1839-1865; (8) Liberty seated type with arrows at date, rays on reverse, issued only in 1853; (9) Liberty seated type with arrows at date (but without rays on reverse), 1854-1855; (10) Liberty seated type with motto IN GOD WE TRUST, 1866-1891; (11) Liberty seated type with motto, with arrows at date (1873-1874); (12) Barber type (designed by Charles E. Barber), 1892-1915; (13) Liberty walking type of 1916-1947; (14) Franklin type of 1948-1963; (15) Kennedy type in silver, 1964; (16) Kennedy type in clad metal, 1965 to date; (17) 1776-1976 bicentennial in copper clad metal; (18) 1776-1976 bicentennial in silver clad metal. Such a set will be very beautiful!

A beautiful type set containing carefully selected coins of excellent quality will be an excellent investment over the years, in my opinion. This has been my often-expressed opinion in the past (in print years ago in the *Empire Investors Report*, *The Forecaster*, my *Coin World* column, and in our own coin company catalogues, for example). If you followed my advice then, you've seen your investment multiply in value. However, "there's no future in the past," as the saying goes—and you are concerned about tomorrow, not yesterday. I think that the outlook for collecting types is very bright and that these represent an excellent way to collect and invest at the same time. I am sure you'll do well!

A Basic Type Set of U.S. Gold Coins

United States gold coins were issued from 1795 through 1933. The series is replete with many rare date and mintmark varieties and many different design types. The following gold coin denominations were issued: $1, $2½, $3, $4, $5, $10, $20, and $50. The $4 denomination was issued in pattern

Different U.S. Half Dollar Designs

1794-1795
The first U.S. half dollar: the "flowing hair" type coined in 1794 and 1795.

1796-1797
The "draped bust type with small eagle reverse" was minted in 1796 and 1797. These are very rare.

1801-1807
The "draped bust type with heraldic eagle reverse" was issued from 1801 to 1807.

1807-1836
The "capped bust type with lettered edge" was produced from 1807 through 1836.

1836-1837
The "small capped bust type with reeded edge and with '50 CENTS' reverse" was made only in two years.

Different U.S. Half Dollar Designs

1838-1839
The "small capped bust type with 'HALF DOL.' reverse" was struck only in 1838 and 1839.

1839-1866
The "Liberty seated type without motto" was made from 1839 to 1866, except for several years.

1853
In 1853 the design with arrows at the date and rays on the reverse was used.

1854-1855
During these two years the with-arrows design was used, but without rays on the reverse.

1866-1891
The "Liberty seated type with motto" (IN GOD WE TRUST) was struck during this period.

Different U.S. Half Dollar Designs

1873-1874
Some varieties of 1873 half dollars and all 1874 halves have arrows at the date.

1892-1915
The "Barber half dollar" style, designed by Charles E. Barber, was made from 1892 to 1915.

1916-1947
The "Liberty walking" half dollar design was used from 1916 until 1947.

1948-1963
From 1948 until 1963 the Franklin half dollar design was produced.

1964 to date
Since 1964, except for the 1776-1976 bicentennial issue (not illustrated), Kennedy half dollars with the heraldic eagle reverse have been made. 1964 issues are of silver; later issues are "clad" metal.

form only; no pieces were ever made for circulation. The $50 denomination was issued by several different California minters (the U.S. Assay Office of Gold being among them) in Gold Rush days, in pattern form by the U.S. government in 1877, and as a commemorative coin for the Panama Pacific International Exposition in 1915. $4 and $50 coins cost thousands of dollars each, so many collectors and investors consider them to be in the realm of the advanced collector or buyer. More important for my present discussion are the issues which are readily available.

$1 gold pieces were minted from 1849 to 1889, $2½ from 1796 to 1929, $3 from 1854 to 1889, $5 from 1795 to 1929, $10 from 1795 to 1933, and $20 from 1849 to 1933. These denominations are generally available to the collector and investor today. Gold $1 pieces are fairly scarce, and $3 pieces are all rare, for these denominations (with the exception of a few dates) were made only in limited numbers, and both denominations were discontinued in 1889. It is surprising to note that the massive $10 and $20 gold coins were often minted by the millions each year—not because they were in demand for circulation in hand-to-hand transactions, but because they formed a convenient monetary unit for bulk bank-to-bank and international transactions. More about this later.

There are several interesting ways a basic gold type set can be formed. Here are some of the most popular:

(1) Set containing one specimen each of the following denominations: $1, $2½, $3, $5, $10, and $20.

(2) Set containing one specimen each of the following denominations minted during the 20th century: $2½, $5, $10, and $20.

(3) Expanded set containing one specimen each of the major designs of the late 19th and early 20th centuries: (1) Gold $1 of the small-diameter type minted from 1849-1854; (2) Gold $1 of the small Indian head or "type II" design minted 1854-1856; (3) Gold $1 of the large Indian head type

United States Gold Coin Type Set

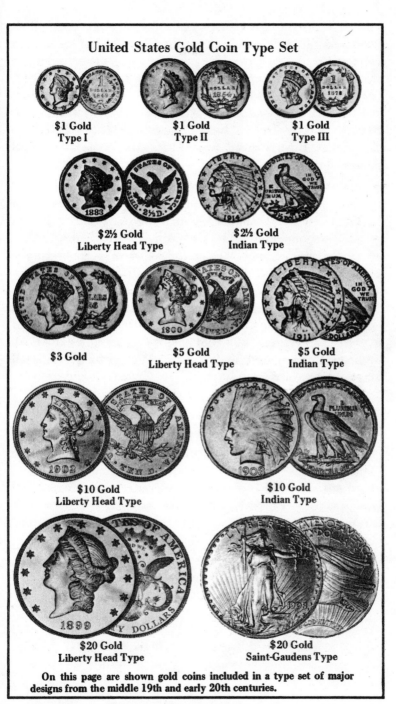

$1 Gold
Type I

$1 Gold
Type II

$1 Gold
Type III

$2½ Gold
Liberty Head Type

$2½ Gold
Indian Type

$3 Gold

$5 Gold
Liberty Head Type

$5 Gold
Indian Type

$10 Gold
Liberty Head Type

$10 Gold
Indian Type

$20 Gold
Liberty Head Type

$20 Gold
Saint-Gaudens Type

On this page are shown gold coins included in a type set of major designs from the middle 19th and early 20th centuries.

minted 1856-1889; (4) $2½ of the Liberty head type minted from 1840 to 1907; (5) $2½ of the Indian head type minted from 1908 to 1929; (6) $3 of the 1854-1889 type; (7) $5 of the 1866-1908 Liberty head type with IN GOD WE TRUST; (8) $5 of the 1908-1929 Indian head type; (9) $10 of the 1866-1907 Liberty head type with IN GOD WE TRUST; (10) $10 of the 1907-1933 Indian head type; (11) $20 of the 1877-1907 Liberty head type; (12) $20 of the 1907-1933 Saint Gaudens type.

Some advice: The spread between the prices of gold coins in worn grades (Very Fine, Extremely Fine, etc.) and Uncirculated grade is much less than it is on copper and silver coins. I recommend acquiring 20th century issues in Uncirculated grades, and leaving the lesser ones to the many buyers who don't know about grade distinctions and/or who are interested in buying the coins for their intrinsic or metallic value. Often the spread is so little that an Uncirculated piece can be obtained for 5% to 10% over the price of a worn 20th century $20 gold piece of a common date. Even a choice Uncirculated piece can be obtained for just a small amount more.

Gold coins are very appealing. There is something indescribably romantic about owning a heavy (about one ounce of gold) $20 piece from years ago.

Investment-wise, gold coins have to be divided into two major categories: (1) those which are rare from a *numismatic* viewpoint, and (2) those which are scarce (for all U.S. gold coins are "scarce") but whose value is dependent more upon the price movement of gold bullion than upon numismatic considerations.

Thus a $3 gold piece, all examples of which are truly rare, is an ideal example of the first category. An Uncirculated specimen of the 1854 $3 gold piece has been valued at the following prices over the years in the *Guide Book of U.S. Coins:* 1948 $27.50, 1953 $35.00, 1958 $77.50, 1963 $245.00, 1968 $350.00, 1973 $650.00, and 1977 $1,750. This amounts to an increase on your investment of 6,264% over the years!

A 1928 $20 gold piece, one of the commonest of all 20th century $20 issues, has had a price movement characteristic of the second category. The price movement of such a coin is more dependent upon the price of gold metal as a commodity. The coin contains about one ounce of gold. As it is a collectors' item it sells for a premium over the bullion price, but the two prices are closely related. The *Guide Book* prices show the following price movements for an Uncirculated 1928 $20 over the years: 1948 $65.00, 1953 $65.00, 1958 $58.50, 1963 $80.00, 1968 $85.00, 1973 $175.00, and 1977 $300. This amounts to an increase over the years of 361%.

My personal recommendation concerning gold coins has been this: if you want the best return on your investment, buy *numismatically rare* gold coins. If you are a commodity specialist or speculator and want to take advantage of world gold price movements, then the "common date" $10 and $20 issues are interesting, but this is an investment in *commodities,* not *numismatics,* and is hence out of the field of this book or, for that matter, my predictions!

A Complete Type Set of U.S. Gold Coins

Gold coins were first minted in 1795. From then until 1933, the last year of coinage, many different design types were issued. The year 1834 represents a turning point in gold coins. In that year the price of gold metal rose to the point at which each coin was worth more than face value. Thus, for example, a group of $5 gold pieces could be melted down, and the gold metal retrieved could be sold back to the Mint for several dollars profit! This caused all 1795-1834 gold coins of the early type to become quite scarce. Most were melted down, including nearly all of certain issues. Mintage figures reveal that 17,796 gold pieces of the $5 denomination were produced in 1822. And yet only three pieces are known today! It is thought that most of the 17,796 were never released, and sometime around 1834 they were melted down.

As a result of the 1834 situation all early United States

gold coins are very rare, and many are extremely rare. Completing a type set of all gold designs thus entails both a generous sum of money and a determined search, for some of the scarcer issues are seldom seen on the market. The *Guide Book of United States Coins* gives an indication of the amount needed to complete a type set of gold coins. However, as is also the case with rare early U.S. copper, nickel, and silver coins, the prices of the rarities are on the low side in this reference. For example, the 1975 edition prices an Uncirculated 1808 quarter eagle at $10,000. I would be happy to pay nearly *twice* that figure for a choice specimen, and I would consider it a bargain!

A reasonable goal in forming a complete collection of the different design types of United States gold coins would be to have the 1795-1834 issues in grades of Very Fine, Extremely Fine, or AU. Later issues can be Uncirculated. When complete, your type set will be a prizewinning display, a set with few equals anywhere in the world!

Chapter 8

Investing
in
Specialized U.S. Coins

In this chapter I tell of ways to invest in and collect specialized United States series. In numismatic parlance this is called "collecting by dates and mintmarks" or "collecting by varieties."

Collecting by dates and mintmarks has always been popular. Indeed, many collectors and investors begin their interest by endeavoring to assemble one of each variety of the current coinage: Lincoln cents, Jefferson nickels, Roosevelt dimes, Washington quarters, Kennedy half dollars, and Eisenhower dollars. Unlike a type collection (which includes but a single specimen of each major design) the specialized collection contains one of each and every variety.

Examples of Specialized Collections

Each series has its specialists. Some numismatists have combined their collecting interests with close study of the coins and have published research articles and books. Often the auction sale catalogue of such a collection will be an important reference book in itself. Over the years James F. Ruddy and I have handled many superb specialized collections. The Armand Champa and Major Lenox R. Lohr collections of U.S. pattern coins were milestones in that field. In fact, the Lohr Collection was the largest and most comprehensive (over 1,500 different pieces) collection of U.S. patterns ever priced and offered for sale. The celebrated collection of U.S. currency formed by Matt Rothert, distinguished past president of the American Numismatic Association, will long be remembered, as will the Terrell Collection of early U.S. half dollars, the Gilroy and Fuller collections of U.S. large cents, and others.

Often the completeness and quality of a choice specialized collection will result in the collection bringing well over current values when it is sold at auction. This compounds the desirability of the investment—the coins, when sold, bring not only their current value, but more! What could be more ideal from an investment viewpoint! This extra reward is an additional compensation for hours of study and patience.

Building a specialized collection of United States coins offers endless opportunities for research. Concentrating on a particular area of coinage will enable you to make many interesting discoveries on your own. In November 1973 our American Auction Association division sold the celebrated collection of United States half dimes formed by Dr. W.E. Caldwell. Dr. Caldwell, a customer and friend for many years, sent us a few paragraphs about his half dimes and the enthusiasm with which he collected them:

"It has been a pleasure to collect the half dimes which you will be selling in your auction. My collecting of this series began quite by accident. I was convalescing from a heart attack when my maid brought in some old coins to see if they were valuable. I laid my paint brushes (my hobby to this point) aside, thank goodness, and borrowed a friend's *Guide Book of United States Coins.*

"I evaluated the small group of miscellaneous coins and bought them. Among these pieces was a well-worn 1837 Liberty seated half dime which had been holed and plugged. This tiny coin brought back memories of an elderly uncle who gave me a nickel for the local Saturday Opera House movies each week when I was a child. I remembered that many of these 'nickels' were half dimes. Why not collect half dimes and see how many different dates I could find? An interesting idea!

"Soon I was off and running—buying half dimes wherever I could find them. One can 'buy in haste and repent in leisure,' and after a few months of fast spending I was many dollars wiser. I found it was desirable to buy from reputable dealers, large auction houses, and at major conventions. It seemed that by this method I could be more sure of getting quality coins, even though a higher price might be required. The 'you get what you pay for' adage is certainly true, and I found this out!

"My collection begins with the 1792 half disme, a coin which certainly is one of the most romantic issues in American numismatics. At one time I had a specimen of each and every half dime variety from 1792 to 1873, but later I traded or sold some of the very worn ones in the hope that I would be able to get top-grade pieces later. It turned out that I was able to do this in some instances but not in others. It is very, very difficult to obtain true Uncirculated examples of the 1794-1805 years, and had this been an absolute requirement there would have been many dates which I would never have acquired. I feel that all Uncirculated half dimes of this era are grossly undervalued, and that examples in grades close to Uncirculated are of extreme rarity in many instances.

"Among the 1829-1837 capped bust half dimes you might find it interesting to know that the 1836 'Small 5c' and the 1837 'Small 5c' varieties are much, much rarer in Uncirculated grade than catalogues indicate. The 1838-O Liberty seated without-stars type is also very undervalued. The specimen that you will be auctioning is the finest I have been able to buy in five years of searching.

"Among later Liberty seated half dimes there are many rarities, particularly in the New Orleans Mint pieces. Many if not most New Orleans half dimes are very weakly struck on the reverse, and to find a sharp strike, if indeed this is possible at all, many specimens must be examined. The most underrated seem to be the 1840-O without drapery, the 1842-O, and the 1844-O. The 1846 Philadelphia Mint half dime is exceedingly rare in higher grades. Another sleeper is the 1848 large date variety in Uncirculated condition. Major rarities are 1849-O, 1852-O, and 1853-O without-arrows variety in better grades.

"The 1859 transitional issue with the reverse of 1860 must rate as one of the most important of all American coin rarities. During the period I formed my collection, the present specimen, the one you will be auctioning, is the only one I was able to buy, and no others were offered for sale in price lists or auctions.

"I can close my eyes and see all of the half dimes in my collection. I hope that the successful bidders on the individual lots will experience the same pleasure I did from these beautiful pieces. While a monetary profit will undoubtedly be realized on the collection, I have profited in what is perhaps an even better way: five years of enjoyable collecting."

When Dr. Caldwell's half dimes were sold a handsome profit was realized. The sale brought record prices and the results exceeded our expectations. As his own words indicate, an additional "profit," the value of which is impossible to estimate in monetary terms, was derived in collecting pleasure.

Over the years James F. Ruddy, I, and the staff of Bowers and Ruddy Galleries have helped many people build specialized collections. In each instance a very attractive profit was realized when the coins were later sold. In each instance the owner has combined investment and collecting to produce a rewarding experience from both a monetary and an enjoyment viewpoint.

What type of specialized collection should you form? This is a question which you can best answer on your own. The possibilities are nearly endless. If you collect pieces in better grades—Uncirculated and Proof for the commoner issues and Fine or better for the rarities—you should do well over the years. Pay attention to quality and value.

Investing in U.S. Silver Dollars

Silver dollars have always been a popular denomination. These massive silver coins have a long and romantic history. Many were minted from Comstock Lode ore and have great historical association with the "Wild West." Added to this is the fact that many 19th century issues can be obtained in Uncirculated condition for low cost.

Silver dollars were first minted in 1794. Early issues are dated from 1794 to 1804, and all are rare. Two of these, the first date and the last, are major rarities. An Uncirculated 1794 dollar was sold for $127,500 in 1974. In the same year Bowers and Ruddy Galleries offered one of the finest known 1804 silver dollars for $200,000. Dates in the intervening years, 1795 through 1803, are valued from several hundred dollars up to several thousand dollars depending on the variety and condition.

Then comes a long gap from 1805 through 1835 with no silver dollar issues. Dollars were made again in 1836, 1838, and 1839—the illustrious and stunningly beautiful pattern issues by mint engraver Christian Gobrecht. These pieces, all of which are very rare, depict the seated figure of Liberty on the obverse and an eagle in flight on the reverse.

From 1840 through 1873 silver dollars were made of the so-called Liberty seated design—an adaptation of the Gobrecht patterns, but with some differences, including a perched eagle rather than a flying eagle on the reverse. Silver dollar coinage was then suspended in 1873.

In 1878 the production of silver dollars was resumed. The Morgan design, by George T. Morgan, made its appearance. This design was continued until it was replaced by the Peace design in 1921.

In 1878 the silver mining interests in the western part of the United States were responsible for the Bland-Allison Act. This legislation provided for the coinage of immense quantities of silver bullion into silver coins, thus providing a ready market—sort of an early-day price support—for silver. The largest silver coin then being minted was the silver dollar, so it was decided to use this denomination to convert bulk silver into coin of the realm.

The result was the minting of hundreds of millions of silver dollars! More silver dollars (over 22,000,000) were minted in the first year, 1878, than in all other previous years (1794 to 1873) of silver dollar coinage combined! There was no commercial need for such a huge quantity of dollars, so nearly all of them went from coinage presses into $1000 mint bags and then right into Treasury vaults for storage. In 1918 the Pittman Act caused 270,232,722 silver dollars to be melted. But still there were enough to go around.

From 1921 through 1935 nearly 200,000,000 Peace-type silver dollars were minted, thus adding to the somewhat depleted (but still healthy) Treasury holdings.

No silver dollars were minted after 1935 (until the Eisenhower dollar in 1971). The appeal of owning a bright Uncirculated silver dollar of the 19th century caused a steady stream of these to flow out of the Treasury vaults. In addition, silver dollars were a popular medium of exchange in Nevada and certain other western states. By the late 1950's word had spread among the public that these "treasures" could be had for face value. In the early 1960's the race was on! Long lines formed at various Treasury outlets as people eagerly purchased silver dollars of long ago—paying just face value for them. The appeal of the situation was enhanced by the occasional finding of scarce and rare dates among the common issues!

When the "Great Treasury Raid," as some writers have called it, was nearly over the Treasury decided to stop selling these old coins. At this point there were slightly over 3,000,000 pieces left, mostly scarce issues made during the 19th century at Carson City, Nevada. After much discussion, the General Services Administration offered these coins for sale in a series of widely-publicized auctions which began in 1972.

The silver dollar situation has been a real windfall for collectors. For about $10 you can buy a silver dollar of the 1870's, 1880's, or 1890's in condition as nice as the day it was minted! Needless to say, this appealing situation has created tens of thousands of collectors of this denomination. Indeed, many collectors and investors have made a specialty of silver dollars alone. The General Services Administration's auction campaign was conducted with posters, leaflets, and advertising in banks, post offices, and elsewhere—and served to create even more interest.

Many investors, collectors, and dealers use the "Mint State System" to grade Uncirculated pieces. This grading system is explained below. MS-60 is equal to an average Uncirculated specimen, MS-65 to a Choice Uncirculated specimen, and MS-70 to a Perfect Uncirculated specimen.

Uncirculated silver dollars and most other coins occur with varying degrees of bagmarks. At the time of striking, they were put into bulk bags for storage. No thought was given to preserving them for future collectors! Even so, it is possible when checking through, say, a bag of 1,000 pieces to find several dozen or so pieces which qualify for Mint State 65 or more.

Here is the Mint State System:

AU = MS-50 to MS-55 on the Sheldon or Mint State scale.

Borderline Uncirculated = MS-56 to MS-59. This is a coin which shows friction or evidence of limited circulation.

Uncirculated = MS-60. "Average" Uncirculated showing bagmarks and other contact marks from the minting and storage process.

Choice Uncirculated = MS-65. A select piece with many fewer than average bagmarks and handling marks, a really outstanding example.

Perfect Uncirculated = MS-70. A perfect piece. Often such an item exists in theory but not in reality, particularly for coins earlier than recent decades.

The collector wanting to achieve a high standard would do well to strive to acquire pieces close to the MS-65 range, for they represent an excellent compromise between high quality and reasonable price. Perfect Uncirculated pieces, when available, are apt to sell for much, much more.

As is often the case with other coin grading systems, the Mint State System is abused now and then. For investment purposes I consider Choice Uncirculated (MS-65) coins to be a happy medium between perfection of grade and the amount you have to pay, as noted earlier. However, when you buy a silver dollar or other coin don't pay an MS-65 price for an MS-60 coin!

Silver dollars will always be one of the most popular United States series. In no other field can so many different varieties of 19th century and early 20th century coins be obtained for such low prices.

United States Commemorative Coins

American commemorative coins were first produced in 1892, in which year specially-designed half dollars were made for distribution at the Columbian Exposition. Commemorative pieces were last made in 1954. Between these years lie a fascinating array of pieces with interesting designs, great historical significance, and high numismatic interest.

Here is a summary of the commemoratives produced. Most commemorative coins have been of the half dollar denomination. From 1892 to 1954 there were 48 different major design types issued. If all date and mintmark varieties are considered, then there are 142 different varieties. Some commemorative half dollars, the 1946 Iowa centennial issue is an example, were issued just in one type or variety. Others were issued in many varieties. As an example of the latter I mention the Arkansas centennial pieces which were issued each year from 1935 to 1939 inclusive (although, strictly speaking, only 1936 was the centennial year), and at three mints (Philadelphia, Denver, and San Francisco) each year.

So, a complete set of Arkansas half dollar varieties consists of three coins from each of five years, for a total of fifteen pieces.

There are two main ways to collect commemorative half dollars: a type set of 48 pieces or a complete variety set of 142 pieces. Which to choose depends upon your budget, for the complete variety set is about twice the price of a type set. Over the years all commemorative half dollars have been excellent investments. However, as mentioned earlier in this book, commemoratives have been subject to speculation from time to time, with resultant ups and downs in prices. The long term trend, however, has been sharply upward.

The two other commemorative silver coins are the 1893 Isabella quarter dollar and the 1900 Lafayette silver dollar.

Nine different varieties of commemorative gold dollars were issued. Events commemorated include the 1922 Grant Memorial, 1915-S Panama Pacific International Exposition, the 1903 Louisiana Purchase Exposition, and the 1904-1905 Lewis and Clark Exposition. All commemorative gold dollars are scarce today. The rarity depends not so much on the mintage as the method of distribution. Hence, 1904-1905 Lewis and Clark issues are much rarer than 1916-1917 McKinley issues, although about 10,000 pieces were issued of each variety. The reason is that most of the Lewis and Clark pieces were sold as souvenirs at the exposition, and thus they were acquired by the public. In the intervening years many have been lost, damaged, or destroyed. By contrast, most of the 1916-1917 McKinley pieces were sold to coin dealers and collectors who saved them carefully.

Commemorative quarter eagles ($2.50 gold pieces) were issued on two occasions: for the 1915 Panama Pacific International Exposition and for the 1926 sesquicentennial (of 150 years of American independence) celebration.

Most spectacular of all commemoratives are the massive $50 gold pieces issued in 1915 and sold at the Panama Pacific

International Exposition. 483 pieces of the round shape and 645 of the octagonal shape were sold. Today these coins are highly desired by numismatists, and the appearance of a choice specimen in an auction sale or other offering is an outstanding event. Pieces are valued at about $15,000 each!

I recommend that all commemoratives that you buy for investment be in choice Uncirculated condition. While circulated pieces and average (with handling marks) Uncirculated coins may go up in value, the choice pieces will always be in the greatest demand.

Diverse Fields of Collecting and Investment

In addition to the standard series of United States coins there are many other numismatic specialties which have attracted collectors and investors in the past. For example, the field of colonial coins does not come to mind when one thinks of investment, but the fact remains that colonial coins have offered some of the finest investment profits to be found anywhere. United States pattern coins are another similar case. Specialists in this field have seen prices double, triple, and then increase again during recent decades.

Generally, investment in a specialized field such as patterns, colonials, paper money, and other off-the-beaten-track series requires more persistence and care than does investment in the standard series. However, if you are willing to take this extra time (or have a trusted dealer do it for you), the rewards can be very great. I recommend consideration of such diverse fields if you can meet the following criteria:

(1) A basic *numismatic* interest (in addition to your investment interest) is helpful and desirable. Most diverse fields of collecting have a high degree of history, romance, and numismatic interest attached to them—and an understanding of this, or a willingness to learn, aids in evaluating which pieces are the best buys, why certain items sell for more than others, and so on. This "requirement" is a plus

factor, I might say—for in my opinion some of the most fascinating coins in all of numismatics are in these fields. So are some of the most fascinating profits!

(2) Patience is required. Actually, two types of patience are required. First, you will find that colonial coins, patterns, rare issues of paper money, and so on are often out of the field of experience of the average coin dealer, so your inquiry might be met with some careless comment such as "I don't know anything about pattern coins, and I never stock them." Of course, this is the dealer's loss! So, some persistence is needed to seek out pieces for purchase. Fortunately, nearly all of the larger numismatic firms maintain stocks (although usually not large ones, due to the rarity of the material) and have such pieces in their auction sales. The second type of patience involves price movements. Prices of many of these pieces do not change on a month-to-month basis. In fact, perhaps a year or two may go by without a price movement. Then there will be a sudden movement—historically upward. Then a year or so of unchanged prices. It is my recommendation that all coin investment be considered as a long term (several years or more) investment, for shorter term investments make money only for dealers—and making money for *you* is what interests you most! With paper money, colonials, and other diverse fields, long-term thinking is essential. However, without exception to my knowledge, any of my customers who built a nice collection of these series five to ten years or more ago can make a tremendous profit by selling today.

(3) Working hand-in-hand with a professional dealer is a "must" in these fields. Without great study it is difficult for the individual investor to keep abreast of all of the varieties and their prices, which items are significant and which aren't, and so on. A trusted dealer is a priceless asset in this regard. The door swings both ways, and you are an asset to the dealer as well—simply because the chances are good that you will give him your "want list" for the pieces you need, or you

will give him an order to buy general or selected pieces for your account.

Investing in Colonial Coins

The coins of colonial America, discussed as a background to the regular United States coins earlier in this book, provide a fertile field for the investor. In recent decades most collectors have placed an emphasis on regular United States mint issues produced from 1793 to the present time. Somewhat neglected have been colonial pieces such as the copper coins of Vermont, Connecticut, Massachusetts, and New Jersey, the silver coins of the Massachusetts Bay Colony, coins honoring President George Washington, and related issues.

The result is that many of these colonial coins can be bought for fractions of the prices of what later American coins of comparable rarity sell for. In the past several years there has been a growing trend toward the collecting of colonial coins—and it is my prediction that the colonial field will have many rarities in the $5,000 to $50,000 range (today there are few colonials which sell for that much), and some which sell for over $100,000 a few years from now. Of course, "a few years from now" is not the time to buy them. The time is now!

Colonial coins, although the interest has not been as great as we think it will be in the future (which, by the way, is an advantage for you as you can buy cheaply now), have indeed done well in the past. A 1652 Pine Tree shilling, a coin valued at $40 in Fine grade in 1948, was valued at over ten times that price in 1977. A 1786 Vermont copper coin of the "Baby Head" variety was valued at $12.50 in Fine grade in 1948. In 1977 such a piece was valued at $550.00 in the *Guide Book*, but a specimen was likely to cost you even more due to their rarity. A 1787 Massachusetts half cent was valued at $4.50 in 1948 and fetches about $60.00 now. The progression of the value of a 1776 Continental dollar in pewter metal in Fine grade is likewise interesting: 1948 $45.00; 1953 $55.00; 1958 $100.00; 1963 $225.00; 1968 $425.00; 1973 $500.00; and 1977 $2250.00. Over the years the Continental dollar has been a collector's favorite, and undoubtedly the trend will continue.

Yes, the field of colonial coins offers many opportunities for the investor. For several thousand dollars a really attractive "portfolio" of these pieces can be acquired.

Investing in Pattern Coins

From 1792 through the late 19th century many varieties of pattern coins were distributed to government officials, collectors, and others. These coins, comprising over 1,500 distinct varieties in all, are avidly collected today. In 1961 James F. Ruddy and I purchased and resold the fabulous collection of United States pattern coins formed by Major Lenox R. Lohr, who was once in charge of the Columbia Broadcasting System and, later, of Chicago's Museum of Science and Industry. This collection, containing nearly every variety of pattern coin known to exist, was the largest such grouping ever to be priced and offered for sale. Included were 7 different patterns of the year 1792 (several of which were the only known specimens of their kind), $4 "Stellas" of 1879 and 1880, many different Gobrecht silver dollars of 1836-1839, and others—all in dazzling array. What were retail prices of that day seem incredible bargains now. It would be my guess that if James F. Ruddy and I had sold the Lohr Collection intact to an investor, that same investor would have seen his money increase in value more than ten times over since then!

The collector and investor willing to take the time to learn about patterns will find this a fertile field for investment. The standard reference book on the subject, *United States Patterns,* by Dr. J. Hewitt Judd, is published in a new edition every several years, with the result that any given edition tends to lag behind the market. The Judd book plus auction

Beautiful U.S. Pattern Coins

This beautiful 1872 pattern twenty dollar gold piece is struck in aluminum! It is from the great Terrell Collection auction sale.

An attractive pattern silver dollar of 1880. Over the years many different designs were tried.

The Amazonian pattern silver dollar of 1872 is considered to be one of the most beautiful of all American coins. This specimen was a highlight of the fabulous collection of Mr. Armand Champa auctioned by us.

Along the right-hand margin are several varieties of pattern one-cent pieces minted in 1858. Over a dozen different designs and die combinations were issued that year!

1877 Pattern Half Dollars — "What Might Have Been"

Regular issue 1877 half dollar of the type struck for circulation.

To the right are four of over a dozen different pattern half dollar designs issued in 1877. To collectors, patterns tell "what might have been" — but wasn't. The study of pattern coins is fascinating. For the investor the pattern field offers great opportunity. Many outstanding rarities—coins of which just a few specimens are known to exist—can be obtained for relatively low sums in comparison to regular issue United States coins.

Over the years Q. David Bowers and James F. Ruddy have bought and sold many of the finest pattern coin collections ever formed. The coins shown here are from the Armand Champa Collection sold at auction by Bowers and Ruddy Galleries. Earlier the Maj. Lenox R. Lohr Collection, a group of over 1,500 coins, was purchased and resold. This was the largest collection of United States pattern coins ever to be priced and offered for sale.

catalogues of leading numismatic firms combine to provide a reasonable amount of pricing information. The several dealers who specialize in patterns can also be of great help to you.

Investing in Major Rarities

For the investor who enjoys the prestige and satisfaction of owning the "rarest of the rare" an investment in recognized rarities of different fields can be very rewarding. During the late 1950's and early 1960's James F. Ruddy and I had several clients, all professional and business men, who were interested in investment for investment's sake—with numismatic interests being secondary. What did we recommend? We suggested that they buy the "rarest of the rare" — important rarities in different series—United States coins, patterns, colonials, territorial gold, and so on.

For James F. Ruddy and me this meant the prestige of being able to buy and resell 1894-S dimes, 1876-CC 20c pieces, MCMVII high-relief gold pieces of 1907, and so on. The investors, most of whom still have their coins (for they have yet to find any other investment field equally or more attractive, so why should they sell?), have done spectacularly well! An investment in the $40,000 to $75,000 range will make one of our clients a millionaire when he sells his holdings!

Today the ownership of prime rarities is an attractive field for the profit-sharing plan or pension fund. Major pieces can be purchased in the $50,000 to $200,000 range, and many are available for even less. The chance to own a "part" of a great rarity is appealing to everyone—and chances are good that participants in such a fund will find much more interest and fascination with a rare coin than with an equivalent amount of common stock, for example. Best of all, the performance of rarities as an investment has been unmatched by other investment fields in recent decades, and I am confident this will continue.

Investing in Paper Money

United States paper money is a large and interesting field. Important categories include:

(1) Colonial currency. Notes issued by the thirteen colonies and by other authorities, including the Continental Congress, during the American colonial period and the early years of independence. These notes are especially interesting because of the unusual designs and mottoes they carry, and because of their immense historical significance. *The Early Paper Money of America,* by Eric P. Newman, is the standard guide to the field.

(2) Broken bank notes and private currency. During the late 18th and early 19th centuries many varieties of currency were issued by private banks, by various states, by merchants and manufacturers, and by others in need of a medium of exchange. Often such notes were redeemable only by the bank or business which issued them. The term "broken bank notes" is used today to cover the field; the term being derived from the fact that most of these early banks and businesses went broke (especially in the Panic of 1837) and their currency issues became worthless. Today, such issues are avidly sought after by collectors. Many interesting varieties, some of which are extremely ornate and artistic, can be purchased for $10 to $20 each. *North American Currency*, by Grover C. Criswell, is the standard reference for this field.

At one time I had a personal interest in obsolete currency of New England from the 1790-1865 years and made a specialty of collecting broken bank notes from this era. I had about 2,000 different varieties, including such unusual denominations as 75c, $1.25, $1.50, $1.75, $3, and $4.

(3) Confederate and southern states currency. Issues of the Confederate States of America during the 1860's and of the related southern states have formed an interesting specialty for many collectors. Many different notes, including extreme rarities, are available for low cost. *Confederate and Southern*

State Currency, by Grover C. Criswell, is the main reference.

(4) Regular United States issues. The Demand Notes of 1861 mark the beginning of United States currency still legal tender today. Earlier U.S. issues such as those released by the Continental Congress and the Bank of the United States were repudiated, and while they are of interest to the collector, they no longer are of interest to the U.S. government!

In 1861 the first Demand Notes were issued. These notes are so-called as they carry the notation "The United States promise to pay to the bearer ——— Dollars on demand." From that time onward many different types of notes were issued. Silver Certificates and Gold Certificates were backed by the respective metals mentioned (this backing has since been repudiated by the U.S. government). Compound Interest Treasury Notes, Interest Bearing Notes, Refunding Certificates, Treasury or Coin Notes, and others were all produced in a wide variety of designs and denominations. From 1863 to 1929 many National Banks in America issued distinctive notes: regular U.S. currency designs (and of legal tender value anywhere in the U.S.A.) but with the name of the issuing bank imprinted. Today these are avidly collected, and many varieties have great value, especially in crisp New (the currency equivalent of "Uncirculated") condition.

From 1861 to 1928 currency was of a size considerably larger than used today. The IBM data-processing card, first made in the early 1920's, was made the size of the paper money of that era so people would find the size easy to use. Now, the IBM cards are still with us, but the large-size currency is long gone. Beginning in 1928 the present-day small-size notes were introduced.

In years gone by some very beautiful currency designs were produced. The high point was reached with the Silver Certificates, Series of 1896. The $1 note portrays an allegorical scene of "History Instructing Youth," the $2 note, a scene of "Science Presenting Steam and Electricity to Commerce and Manufacture," and the $5 note (the largest in the 1896 series), an untitled scene showing the Goddess of

The Beautiful "Educational" Notes of 1896

$1 "Educational" Silver Certificate of 1896. The scene depicts "History Instructing Youth." Such notes have been a superb investment over the years.

$2 "Educational" Silver Certificate of 1896 depicting "Science Presenting Steam and Electricity to Commerce and Manufacture."

$5 "Educational" Silver Certificate of 1896 illustrating the Goddess of Electricity as the dominant force in the world.

Electricity as the dominant force in the world. Other magnificent designs are found throughout the series of large-size notes from 1861 onward. Unfortunately, this artistry was not continued with the small-size notes. Perhaps someday the Treasury will think again in terms of artistry in addition to utility. Really, the two can make a perfect combination.

Collector interest in large- and small-size notes and also in fractional currency (smaller notes of 3c to 50c values issued after the Civil War when coins were scarce in circulation) has been great in recent years. There are several excellent reference books available. These include *Paper Money of the United States* by Robert and Jack Friedberg, *U.S. Large Size Paper Money 1861-1923*, by William Donlon, and the *Hewitt-Donlon Catalog of U.S. Small Size Paper Money*. The Society of Paper Money Collectors provides an international forum for collectors and investors interested in all fields of paper money.

In my opinion, paper money of all kinds offers attractive investment opportunities. Perhaps foremost in this regard, due primarily to the ease of collecting specimens, are the United States notes from 1861 to date, although interesting opportunities exist in other paper money fields as well. Colonial currency in particular would seem to be under-valued, in my opinion.

For investment purposes I would recommend acquiring United States notes in strictly New condition, without folds, soiling, or other evidence of wear. Most popular today, and probably most popular in the future, are the issues of lower denominations: $1, $2, $5, and $10—particularly of scarce "types" (as opposed to rare signature combinations). Beauty is always attractive, and the more beautiful notes (the 1896 Silver Certificates are a case in point) will always rank high in collector interest. A complete set of $1, $2, and $5 "Educational" notes of the 1896 Silver Certificate series now costs about $3,500. In the first edition of this book I noted that such a set then cost $1,000 (this was in 1974), and wrote "I predict this set will double in value within five years."

Popular U.S. Paper Money Varieties

This design of National Currency is known as the "Lazy 2" variety, for the 2 is laying on its side! In high grades these are very scarce.

$5 note featuring Chief Onepapa. This beautiful design has always been a paper money collectors' favorite.

The "numismatic reverse" of a $5 note of 1886. Illustrated are five silver dollars of that year! In the past there have been many stunningly beautiful currency designs.

Diverse Types of U.S. Paper Money

1922 Gold Certificate

Above and right: Fractional currency notes from the collection of Mr. Matt Rothert, distinguished past president of the American Numismatic Association.

Authentic $3 bill from the 19th century.

Chapter 9

Investing in Gold Coins

Introduction to Gold Coins

Gold has always had a fascination for mankind. From ancient times to the present gold has had an allure, a romance unmatched by any other metal.

Throughout history the highest-valued coins of the realm have been struck in gold. In recent centuries this precious metal has been the foundation of the world's monetary system. Paper money currency systems come and go, but gold holds its value.

Gold coins have a special charm: they represent the world's most famous, most desired metal in a convenient and artistic form. One can only read about the bars of gold bullion in Fort Knox or in the Bank of England, but one can actually *hold* and *own* a gold coin.

Paper francs and marks and cruzieros and dollars and pounds may rise and fall in value. The holder of German paper marks during the 1920's found that a bushel basket of currency would not buy a loaf of bread. The holder of United States Gold Certificates, "guaranteed in gold" obligations, and other pieces of paper found that they were just that: pieces of paper—when the United States government decided to dishonor all of its gold obligations (this happened in the early 1930's). Most other countries have experienced similar situations. Aware of the stability of gold, many governments have tried to legislate against the ownership of gold. Did you know, for example, that in the United States, a country renowned for its freedoms, it was illegal until December 31, 1974 to own a small bar of gold metal? Fortunately, in most world areas it is not illegal to own gold coins. Therein lies an opportunity.

As noted earlier, there are two basic reasons to collect or invest in gold coins. First is investment from a numismatic viewpoint. Second is investment from a metallic or intrinsic value viewpoint. Investors in both areas have done well over the years. The numismatic gold investors have done *extremely* well!

Gold Coins of the United States

Throughout colonial times gold coins of other countries, particularly of Spain and Great Britain, circulated in America and were used in large commercial transactions. As I mentioned earlier in this book, the first United States gold coins were minted in 1795; pieces of the $5 and $10 denominations. From then until gold coins were last minted in 1933, hundreds of millions of individual pieces were produced.

Standard gold denominations are: $1, $2½, $3, $5, $10, and $20. The basic American gold coin value was the "eagle" or $10 gold coin, first minted in 1795. Later, when $20 gold coins were made for circulation beginning in 1850 they were called "double eagles." Today, numismatists adhere to these same terms. The $2½ is called a "quarter eagle" and the $5, a "half eagle." There are no special terms for the $1 and $3 issues.

In 1879 and 1880 a number of pattern $4 gold coins were produced. One 1879 issue was minted to the extent of 415 pieces, a rather large issue for a pattern coin, so that specimens could be available for congressmen, newspaper editors, and other influential people. The $4 gold pieces, called "Stellas" (from the five-pointed star on the reverse), are numismatic prizes today. A choice Proof example of one of the "common" 1879 issues, the style with Miss Liberty in

Early United States Gold Coins

1796 $2½ gold (quarter eagles). The variety at the left has no stars on the obverse. The specimen at the right has stars.

1795 and 1805 $5 gold pieces (half eagles). 1795, with the reverse eagle on a palm branch, is the first year of issue.

Later styles are typified by these $5 pieces of 1812 and 1818. Note the head is smaller on the 1812 type.

Early $10 "eagles." 1795 is the first year of issue. The 1797 illustrates the heraldic eagle reverse.

a flowing hair style, brings over $20,000 today, and rare varieties of 1879 and 1880 sell for considerably more when they are offered in the numismatic marketplace.

$50 gold coins were produced as patterns by the Philadelphia Mint in 1877. In 1915 the San Francisco Mint struck a small number of $50 pieces, some of round shape and others octagonal, as commemoratives to be sold at the Panama Pacific International Exposition held in San Francisco that year. The coins were sold for twice face value, or $100 each. Today each coin is valued at over $15,000!

During the early years of our republic gold coins were used in settlement of large transactions, particularly to distant places. Prior to 1861 the American currency system was hectic, and few people placed any trust in the millions of notes issued by private banks. Gold was *the* store of value.

Following the establishment in 1861 of the United States paper money system as we know it, the public became more and more confident of paper money (often called "fiat currency," for its value depends on the faith of the government issuing it, rather than any intrinsic value) and dependence on gold coins declined. Gold coins were rarely seen in circulation after the mid-19th century. However, the quantities of gold coins minted actually increased during this period. Gold pieces were minted by the millions. Most were stored in Treasury or bank vaults or were shipped overseas in settlement of international transactions. As an example, in the year 1928 there were 8,816,000 $20 gold pieces minted! In face value this amounted to $176,320,000! During the same year the total combined face value of the coins commonly used in circulation—U.S. coins from cents through silver dollars (although even silver dollars were not used actively)—amounted to just $11,617,319—a tiny fraction of the 1928 $20 coinage.

What happened to all of the 1928 $20 and the hundreds of millions of other gold coins minted over the years? As I mentioned earlier (refer to page 129), most gold coins of the

$20 Gold Double Eagles

MCMVII (1907) high relief $20 gold. This design by Augustus Saint-Gaudens, the noted sculptor, is one of America's most artistic. Just 11,250 of these beautiful coins were minted. Later issues have the date in regular (Arabic) figures.

1850 $20 of the 1849-1866 type without motto; and 1873-CC (Carson City) $20 of the 1866-1876 type with IN GOD WE TRUST and TWENTY D.

1884-CC $20 of the 1877-1907 type with TWENTY DOLLARS on reverse; and 1925-D $20 of the 1907-1933 Saint-Gaudens type in shallow relief.

1795-1834 era were melted down around the latter year when the intrinsic value of gold coins exceeded their face value. Except for losses due to casualties and recall by the government of earlier issues (such as the obsolete $1 and $3 denominations), most gold coins minted from 1834 through 1933 were still in existence during that latter year. In 1933 the United States went off of the gold standard, and the ownership of gold coins by the public (but not including numismatists) was made illegal. Gold coins held by the Treasury, by banks, and by the public were called in and were melted into gold bullion. Once this had been accomplished, the United States government raised the price of gold bullion from $20.67 an ounce to $35.00—thus making a fantastic profit at the expense of the citizens and banks who received only face value for their coins. Immediately a $20 gold piece, worth just $20 early in 1933, became worth $35!

During the late 19th and early 20th centuries tremendous quantities of American gold coins, particularly of the $5, $10, and $20 denominations, were shipped overseas in settlement of international transactions. When the Gold Order of March, 1933 was declared, foreign governments gave no thought to returning their $20 gold pieces and other coins to the U.S. government in exchange for "greenbacks." If anything, they held on to their gold coins even more tightly!

This had a very fortunate sequel. When collecting gold coins became popular, Switzerland (in particular) became the number one source for gold coins in quantities. From deep within Swiss bank vaults came millions of American gold coins, many of them in Uncirculated condition! It is from Swiss banks and other overseas sources that most so-called "common date" gold coins have been acquired in recent years. Although the Swiss holdings have included some rarities as well, most classic rarities remained in coin collections in America (there was no requirement to turn rarities into the government for melting in 1933). Thus the gold coins available for collecting and investment today are comprised of a combination of rarities from old-time collections plus other issues, usually of the $5, $10, and $20 denominations, which have been imported from Switzerland and other countries in recent years.

Regular-issue United States gold coins can be collected in a number of ways. I earlier discussed the formation of type sets of United States gold coins—one of the most interesting ways to form an attractive investment group of these pieces. Gold coins can be collected by date and mintmark sequence as well. James F. Ruddy and I have helped a number of clients build sets of $20 gold pieces from 1850 through the last collectable date in the series, 1932, sets of gold dollars from 1849 through 1889, and so on. Building these sets is always a challenge, and without exception each has produced a handsome profit for the client who purchased it.

Rare United States gold coins have done extremely well as an investment over the years. Here are a few examples:

An 1851 gold dollar in Uncirculated grade, valued at $7.50 in 1948, catalogued $350.00 in 1977—for an increase of 4,566% in the investment! Even more spectacular has been the performance of an 1855 gold dollar, an example of the scarce so-called "type II" design (minted 1854-1855). An Uncirculated 1855 catalogued $12.50 in 1948. By 1977 the catalogue value had risen to $2,100—for an increase of 16,700%! An 1807 Uncirculated $2½ piece went from $100 to $5,700 in the same period; a Proof 1879 $4 Stella from $500 to $20,000, and a 1907 MCMVII $20 high relief in Uncirculated grade went from $110 to $4,400. Gold coins of exceptional numismatic value were indeed spectacular investments! Gold coins of high intrinsic value but of moderate scarcity also did well, but not so well as their rarer brothers. For an example, an Uncirculated 1928 $20 gold piece, a so-called "common date" (and the example I cited earlier), went from $65 catalogue value to $300, for a gain of "just" 361%.

Related to regular United States gold issues are the

"territorial" or "pioneer" pieces. Throughout American history there have been a number of important gold discoveries. As these were made at locations distant from United States mints at the time, often private assayers and bankers produced coins from the newly-found metal. Christopher Bechtler and August Bechtler operated a private mint at Rutherfordton, North Carolina, during the early 19th century. All of the Bechtler issues are scarce and are in great demand today. In 1849 $5 and $10 gold pieces were issued by the Oregon Exchange Company. These coins, extremely rare today, depict a beaver on the obverse and were made from gold found in the Oregon Territory. In Salt Lake City, Utah, the Mormons produced gold coins from 1849 through 1860. These were issued in the denominations of $2½, $5, $10, and $20. In Colorado during the 1860's several firms produced gold coins. The most famous of these was Clark, Gruber & Co., some of whose coins depicted Pikes Peak on the obverse.

Most spectacular of all territorial or pioneer gold coins are the issues produced in California following the discovery of gold there in January 1848. The large $50 gold pieces, mostly of octagonal shape, were popularly designated as "slugs," supposedly because several of these made an ideal weapon when wrapped in a handkerchief! These massive gold coins are extremely rare today. The rarity, romantic appeal, and historical association of these pieces combine to make $50 California gold coins among the most desirable of all American issues.

Over the years territorial gold coins have been excellent investments. For the investor who can afford them (for even the most "common" issues are apt to cost $500 to $1000 each, and rarities sell for many thousands of dollars), these issues combine investment and romance in a very desirable way.

Territorial Gold Coins

$2½ Georgia Gold
Templeton Reid, Assayer

$50 Gold "Slug"
Augustus Humbert
(U.S. Assayer of Gold)
California, 1851

1860 Mormon $5 Gold
Salt Lake City, Utah

1860 $20 Pikes Peak Gold
Clark, Gruber & Co., Denver

1849 $5 Gold
Oregon Exchange Co.
Oregon Territory

$20 U.S. Assay Office of Gold
California, 1853

$50 Gold "Slug"
U.S. Assay Office of Gold

Gold Coins of the World

When the United States went off of the gold standard in 1933 many other countries still adhered to the time-honored tradition of minting gold coins. Certain countries still produce gold coins today, although this production is mainly for special issues (such as commemoratives), rather than for pieces which find wide use as a circulating medium.

There are several ways to invest in and collect gold coins of the world. The standard reference on the series, *Gold Coins of the World,* by Robert and Jack Friedberg, provides a guide to the general types minted from 600 A.D. to the present. For date and mintmark varieties it is necessary to consult specialized books pertaining to individual countries.

Collecting one gold coin from as many different countries as possible is a popular method of collecting and investing. As might be expected, this interest has sharply focused demand on certain gold coins from obscure countries—the 10-mark and 20-mark 1895 gold coins of German New Guinea being excellent examples. In Uncirculated grade each of these coins is worth several thousand dollars—simply because these two issues are the only gold coins ever produced for this country (which was in existence under that name only from 1894 until the end of World War I.)

It is interesting to note that Newfoundland, a province of Canada, circulated its own gold coins from 1865 through 1888 inclusive. These pieces were of the unusual denomination of $2. Eight different varieties were produced during that span of years.

Likewise popular, and likewise a good investment in the past, are Canadian $5 gold pieces minted from 1912 to 1914, $10 gold pieces minted during the same years, and a series of gold sovereigns (of the same approximate size as the $5 gold piece but of different design) minted from 1908 through 1919.

Very popular with collectors in the United States are the large and very impressive-appearing Mexican 50-peso gold pieces minted with dates from 1921 through 1947 inclusive. A complete collection of dates of these pieces, each of which is larger than a United States $20 gold piece, comprises issues of the years 1921 through 1931 inclusive and 1943 through 1947 inclusive—16 different dates in all.

The area of dates and mintmarks has not been fully researched, and new discoveries are constantly being made as collector interest in world gold coins increases. An interesting example of this was Lot No. 1939 in our sale of the Matt Rothert Collection in November 1973.

This coin, a part of the collection acquired over a long period of years by Mr. Rothert, was described as: "1915 P.V.G. 1 Libra. Friedberg No. 73; Harris 60. Rare, possibly unique specimen of this date with initials P.V.G. Harris lists this date as 'rare' and notes that it is unconfirmed, meaning that no specimens were known to him at the time of his compilation. Such an opportunity will elicit spirited bidding competition. Choice Brilliant Uncirculated condition."

The coin sold for $875.00. The point of all this? Mr. Rothert acquired it years earlier as a "common" $5-size gold coin of Peru and paid probably $15 to $30 for it! The coin was a wonderful investment for Mr. Rothert. Chances are good that it will be a wonderful investment for its new owner, too—for who can argue that $875 is "too high" for a coin of which perhaps one or just a few specimens are known?

While there are many investment possibilities among world gold coins, care should be exercised in the purchase of them for many have been restruck or unofficially produced. To fill the demand for British sovereigns, French Napoleons, and even U.S. $20 gold pieces, private "mints" in Lebanon, Italy, and elsewhere have produced a flood of coins. During a recent trip to Europe I visited a "gold coin exchange" operated by a leading bank. I was appalled to see that not one of the nearly 100 gold coins shown was genuine! I asked how well these were selling and was told, "Very well, as many people want to invest in gold coins now."

When buying gold coins, or any rarities for that matter, it makes good sense to buy from an established rare coin dealer with impeccable professional credentials. For example, dealer members of the International Association of Professional Numismatists and the Professional Numismatists Guild guarantee the authenticity of the items they sell.

Investing in Common-Date Gold Coins

All gold coins are basically scarce by comparison to smaller denominations of a given country. However, there are some which are known as "common gold" issues, simply because the coins, while scarce in a relative sense, are common within their own series. For example, the 1928 $20 gold piece, to use my earlier illustration again, is a common date. The price movement of such a coin tends to be more influenced by the current world market price of gold bullion than by numismatic considerations.

The 1928 $20 gold piece (or any U.S. $20) contains .967 ounce of gold. Thus, if the bullion price of gold is $40 per ounce, the $20 piece contains $38.68 worth of this precious metal. If the gold price is $50 per ounce, the $20 is worth $48.37 from a metallic value, and so on. As the coin has numismatic value as well, the price of a 1928 $20 is always over the bullion or melt-down value. As an example, in early 1977 when gold was at about $135 per ounce, a 1928 Brilliant Uncirculated $20 sold for about $275 to $300. Worn pieces sold for less.

Popular with investors who desire a high metallic value are the following world gold coin issues: Austria 4-ducats (.443 oz. pure gold), Austria 100-corona (.980 oz.), Belgium 20-francs (.187 oz.), Colombia 5-pesos (.235 oz.), France 20-francs (.187 oz.), England 1-pound or sovereign (.235 oz.), Hungary 20-krona (.196 oz.), Mexico 50-pesos (1.206 oz.), Mexico 10-pesos (.241 oz.), Mexico 5-pesos (.121 oz.), Mexico 2½-pesos (.060 oz.), Mexico 2-pesos (.048 oz.), Netherlands 10-guilders (.195 oz.), Peru 1-libra (.235 oz.),

Russia 5-rubles (.124 oz.), Switzerland 20-francs (.187 oz), U.S.A. $20 (.967 oz.), U.S.A. $10 (.484 oz.), and U.S.A. $5 (.242 oz.).

Prices of common-date world gold coins move in relation to the price of gold bullion and also in relation to international monetary and political crises. Our previously-mentioned common 1928 Uncirculated $20 gold piece has catalogued for the following amounts over the years: 1948 $65.00, 1953 $65.00, 1958 $58.50, 1963 $80.00, 1968 $85.00, 1973 $175.00, and 1977 $300.00—for an overall price appreciation of 361%. Taken on its own, this increase in value (expressed another way, the 1977 price is 361% of the 1948 price) has resulted in the coin's having been a really fine investment.

In the past, investment in common date gold coins has appealed mainly to the investor interested in hedging against the depreciation of the U.S. dollar and, at the same time, taking advantage of the price rise in gold bullion. It is abundantly evident that the price rises over the years are very modest in comparison to the profits from *numismatically rare* pieces, but nevertheless there has been an attractive profit.

My recommendations are:

(1) If you are mainly interested in hedging against the value of the dollar and if you are interested in the price fluctuation of gold bullion, then common date gold coins provide an interesting way of participating in this. I think that the best profits are to be found with *numismatically rare* coins, but I also realize that it is natural for an investor to want to diversify. Bear in mind that the values of common date gold coins have tended to fluctuate (move up and down) whereas the values of numismatically rare gold coins have a reasonably steady trend upward. If you want to invest in gold metal, then common date gold coins are ideal for this.

(2) However, if you do invest, I recommend paying a small additional premium to buy Uncirculated coins. Most sales of

common date gold coins are by "sales organizations," not established rare coin dealers, and their customers for the most part don't know about coin grading. This is an advantage for you, for it means that Uncirculated pieces can be obtained for just a little more than it takes to buy worn coins. By buying Uncirculated coins you will then have two future markets: the common date gold coin market and also the numismatic market. This gives you a double market for just slightly added cost.

Chapter 10

Investing

in

Coins of the World

Coins of the world—coins of countries other than the United States—have always been popular with collectors. While most collectors and investors begin their interest with United States issues, often coins of other countries soon attract their interest.

The scope of world coins is as unlimited as the world itself. Perhaps indicative of this are the figures given in the front of the *Standard Catalog of World Coins,* by Chester Krause and Clifford Mishler. This book, which *only* covers coins from approximately 1850 to the present time, features pieces from 261 different countries, including over 30,000 coins listed by individual dates! When you consider that the years from 1850 to date comprise but a fraction of the world's total coinage, you can see that the field is virtually endless!

No one has ever attempted to collect one of each and every date and mintmark from every country in the world. To do this would require several lifetimes, not to mention King Midas' treasury! So, collectors and investors tend to specialize.

Crowns or Silver Dollars of the World

One popular specialty is to collect dollar-size coins of the world—coins generally known as "crowns." Most countries issued such pieces. These can be gathered in a number of ways. Obtaining a silver-dollar size coin from one each of as many different countries as possible is an interesting challenge. Did you realize, for example, that Hawaii was once an independent country (Kingdom of Hawaii) and issued its own coinage, including silver dollars? An 1883 Hawaiian silver dollar in Choice Uncirculated condition can be obtained for about $2,000. How has such a coin performed as an investment? The answer: in 1971 we were selling these for about $400 each, and several years before that we offered them in the $150 to $200 range. They have been a wonderful investment for those who have owned them.

Just as is true in the United States series, certain coins of the world are rare and others are common. As an investor you will be mainly interested in coins of proven scarcity and rarity in fields which are popular or which may become popular in the future. Thus, the 1883 Hawaiian dollar has been an excellent investment for it is a "key" item—the only silver-dollar size coin ever officially issued by the Kingdom of Hawaii.

Popular with many collectors and investors are many of the silver dollar issues of our neighbor to the north, Canada. In 1935 the Canadian government commenced issuing an illustrious series of silver dollars. These large and impressive coins have been used over the years to commemorate various historical events. The standard silver dollar design portrays the British monarch (King George V in 1935 and 1936, King George VI from 1937 to 1952, and Queen Elizabeth II from 1953 to date) on the obverse and an Indian and a fur trapper in a canoe on the reverse. Interspersed among these regular issues are a number of special designs.

The 1939 Canadian silver dollar features a reverse motif depicting the Canadian Parliament buildings. The 1949 issue shows a fully-rigged sailing ship emblematic of Newfoundland. The 1958 Canadian dollar bears a distinctive totem pole on the reverse and commemorates the centennial of the Canadian province of British Columbia. The 1964 issue observes the centennial of Charlottetown, Quebec and has its own descriptive design. Other interesting issues throughout the silver dollar series entice the collector. As is true of United States silver dollars, some Canadian silver dollars are

Crowns of Great Britain

Over the centuries Great Britain has produced many beautiful crowns. The approximate size of a silver dollar, these coins are favorites with collectors. On this page are shown several interesting varieties:

1703 issue with "VIGO" below the portrait of Queen Anne. This romantic coin was struck from Spanish silver treasure captured by the British naval forces in the harbor of Vigo, Spain. This crown commemorates the event!

1845 crown depicting Queen Victoria (who ascended to the throne in 1837) as a young girl. Crowns of this design were first minted in 1839.

The beautiful "Gothic crown" was minted in 1846, 1847, and 1853. Most known specimens are of the 1847 date. The one illustrated here is the exceedingly rare 1846 from our Terrell Collection auction sale.

Only 932 specimens were minted of the rare 1934 crown—making it one of the world's greatest modern scarcities.

rare and others are common. The 1948, a recognized rarity, sells for over one thousand dollars in choice Uncirculated condition. On the other hand, many issues of recent years—issues which are very common—sell for just a few dollars each. Investment-wise, the scarcer and rarer dates are the best buys, in my opinion. Purchase only choice Uncirculated specimens. For investment purposes, it is better to have one choice Uncirculated example than four or five Extremely Fine pieces—at least for my money.

Crowns of Great Britain have always been popular with collectors and investors. Scarcer issues have appreciated in value dramatically over the years. The series of British crowns is a long and illustrious one. The earliest issue to bear a date was struck in the year 1551. Since then many different varieties have been produced. Most bear the portrait of the reigning king or queen on the obverse. The reverse usually depicts a heraldic motif or an allegorical scene (such as the popular St. George and the dragon design).

In particular demand by collectors are the issues of the 19th and 20th centuries, beginning with the first crown of Queen Victoria, a coin issued in 1839. In 1847 a particularly beautiful design, the "Gothic crown," was produced. The obverse and reverse of this piece have the legend in ornate Gothic letters. Examples of this design were struck, although in severely restricted numbers, in 1846 and 1853 as well. Today the Gothic crown is a favorite with collectors. As is the case with most other British crowns, Gothic crowns have been an excellent investment. A piece which cost $20 or $30 twenty years ago sells for fifty times that price today!

Among 20th century crowns, the issues of King George V have always been popular. These were produced from 1927 through 1936, but only in small numbers—with the exception of the 1935 Jubilee commemorative. The rarest issue, 1934, is a coin of which only 932 pieces were minted!

In 1937 in anticipation of the impending coronation of the Prince of Wales, soon to become King Edward VIII, a

1937 King Edward VIII Crown

Acquired by Bowers and Ruddy Galleries and subsequently sold by the firm in 1976, the 1937 silver five-shilling or crown piece is the world's most valuable "silver dollar." In one of the greatest love stories of all time the heir to the throne, about to become King Edward VIII, abdicated the throne of Great Britain in order to marry Mrs. Wallis Warfield Simpson.

series of coins bearing the portrait of King Edward VIII were prepared. These pieces included denominations of farthing (¼ of a penny), halfpenny, penny, brass threepence, sixpence, shilling, florin (equal in value to two shillings), halfcrown, and crown. The only examples which were released into the hands of the public were some of the brass threepence pieces. It is not known how many of these were distributed, but guesses range from one dozen to two dozen specimens. In 1963 James F. Ruddy and I purchased one of these rare 1937 King Edward VIII threepence pieces and sold it into the magnificent collection of Mr. Carl Nickel of Calgary, Alberta, Canada—who then considered it to be the centerpiece of his collection.

It is interesting to note that the Duke of Windsor, whose abdication from the throne of England was part of what is perhaps the greatest love story of all time, searched for years for a specimen of a coin bearing his portrait as King. Finally he was able to obtain one of the brass threepence pieces through a coin dealer in America.

One of the most astounding finds of my numismatic career occurred a few years ago when our firm purchased six different official British coins bearing the portrait and inscription of King Edward VIII. These coins, subsequently sold by us in 1976, of various denominations from the farthing to the large crown, were said to have been the property of Mr. Paget, who designed the obverse of the coins for the Royal Mint in London. Certainly the 1937 King Edward VIII silver-dollar size crown coin is one of the world's most valuable, romantic, and rare issues!

The field of crowns or silver-dollar size coins of the world offers as many variations in design and craftsmanship as there are individual countries. Many small countries, now part of larger countries or otherwise lost to modern political geography, are commemorated by coins. Take for example German New Guinea. This country became part of the German colonial empire in 1894. It was ruled under German auspices until the end of World War I, at which time it was turned over to Australia for administration and guidance. German New Guinea issued coins only in 1894 and 1895. One of these, the 5-mark piece, is of crown or silver-dollar size. The obverse depicts a beautiful bird of paradise in resplendent glory. The scarcity and beauty of this coin, combined with the fact that it is the only crown-size coin of this former country, have made the 1894 crown a "blue chip" with collectors and investors for many decades. Coins like this will always be in demand!

Likewise renowned for its beauty and rarity is the splendid 1925 one-quetzal crown of Guatemala. This lovely coin depicts a quetzal bird on the obverse and reverse. It has always been an important coin, and over the years choice specimens have been wonderful investments.

Mexico, our neighbor to the south, has issued crown-size coins for many years. The sheer variety and number of dates and mintmarks issued exceed our own United States coins. Fourteen different mints, each with its own distinctive mintmark, produced coins in Mexico over a period of time. In addition, there were many unofficial issues produced by revolutionaries and insurgents.

In early times the Mexican monetary system was the same as the Spanish and was divided into the real—with multiples and fractions. A real was 1/8th of a dollar, or 12½c in United States money. 12½c pieces were known as "bits." Our present term "two bits" is from the days in America when two-real or two-bit coins were in circulation (a two-bit piece being worth 25c). The dollar-size Mexican coin of the 1700's and 1800's was of the eight-real denomination. Known also as "pillar dollars," early issues of the 8-real denomination have been honored in many stories of pirate and treasure lore. Such coins were legal tender in the United States until 1857.

In later years the peso was adopted as the standard for a silver-dollar size coin. Many interesting varieties, including some with commemorative motifs, have been produced in

Interesting Crowns of the World

GUATEMALA
1824
8 reales

SWITZERLAND
1812
40 Batzen
of
Vaud

MEXICO
1738
8 reales
"Pillar
Dollar"

JAPAN
1882
1 yen

Interesting Crowns of the World

AUSTRIA 1698 taler of Leopold "The Hogmouth"

GERMANY 1772 taler from Frankfurt

FRANCE 1811 5 francs of Napoleon

GERMANY 1913 pattern 5 marks of Bavaria

recent decades. The Mexican currency has depreciated over the years so far as face value is concerned. So, when a silver-dollar size coin was made in 1968 to commemorate the XIX Olympics it bore a value not of one peso but of 25 pesos!

The country of Switzerland has produced many magnificent crown-size coins in recent centuries. Perhaps the most famous of these are the so-called "shooting talers"— dollar-size coins used to commemorate shooting festivals held by sportsmen in that alpine land. Examples are the coins issued for the 1842 festival in Chur, Switzerland, the 1855 festival in Solothurn, the 1857 festival in Bern, the 1859 event in Zurich, and the 1876 gathering in Lausanne. There are many other issues as well.

In recent years a number of countries have capitalized on collector interest for crown-size coins and have produced pieces in large quantities for sale to numismatists. By comparison, the surviving quantities of very early crown issues, especially those in better grades of condition, are very small. The earlier pieces have been excellent investments in the past, and with the worldwide interest in coin collecting I believe they will be excellent investments in the future. As guidelines, I recommend that you select pieces of better grades, emphasize "type" pieces (as opposed to rare subvarieties), and diversify your investment among at least several different countries.

Minor Coins of the World

Classified as "minor coins" are pieces of less than crown or dollar size. Such coins circulated as the small change within the currency system of a given country. Just as American numismatists collect Lincoln cents and Jefferson nickels by date and mintmark varieties, collectors of other countries often aspire to complete date and mint sets of centimes, kroner, centavos, and other minor denominations. Due to the vast number of issues produced in past centuries, the market for rare dates and mintmarks will be necessarily mainly confined to numismatists within that country. To be sure, there are some exceptions: American numismatists are avid collectors of Canadian, British, and Mexican coins by dates and mintmarks, for example. However, it is true to say that the main market for centime pieces by date and mint is with French numismatists, the main market for pfennigs by date and mint is with German collectors, and so on.

Often the number of varieties can be quite extensive. For example, German mints since 1850 comprise nearly a dozen locations, as indicated by the following mintmarks: "A" for Berlin, "B" for Hannover (until 1878), "B" for Vienna (1938-1945 only), "C" for Frankfurt, "D" for Munich, "E" for Dresden, "F" for Stuttgart, "G" for Karlsruhe, "H" for Darmstadt, and "J" for Hamburg. Considering all of these mints, the number of coins produced is simply tremendous. To cite but a random example, the collector of one-mark coins (a mark is a silver coin about the size of a U.S. quarter dollar) would for the year 1874 have the following varieties to gather: 1874-A, 1874-B, 1874-C, 1874-D, 1874-E, 1874-F, 1874-G, and 1874-H!

Often a mint produced coins for many different countries. Perhaps the world's most prolific mint in terms of internationality was the Heaton Mint in Birmingham, England. This mint produced coins, usually designated by an "H" mintmark, for many different countries throughout the British Empire, including dozens of Canadian issues. The Heaton Mint, privately owned, also produced many pieces for Great Britain, especially during times when the facilities of the Royal Mint were extremely busy. Another interesting private mint in England is the curiously-named King's Norton Mint, which produced English pennies during the years of 1918 and 1919. These coins, designated as 1918-KN and 1919-KN, were made in relatively small numbers and are highly desired by collectors today.

In 1904 a tiny coin appeared in Panama; a coin scarcely the size of an aspirin tablet and with a value of 2½ centesimos. Made of silver, this coin is affectionately known as the "Panama pill." The curiosity value of this piece has made it a favorite with collectors. This illustrates another point: often items with a "story" or with some particularly unusual feature are in great demand by collectors.

Throughout the panorama of world coins there are many pieces with interesting stories. Such historical associations often make pieces popular with collectors, even though the same collectors would not otherwise seek after these coins. Interesting examples are the 1929 puffin and half-puffin issues of the island of Lundy. In 1925 Mr. Martin Coles Harman, a businessman from London, purchased this small island which is situated off the coast of the southern part of England. In 1929 he produced these small coins as souvenirs and for circulation in his private empire. Produced mainly as a curiosity, the pieces were given the denominations of puffin and half-puffin, the puffin being a bird indigenous to that lonely isle. In April 1930 the British government fined Mr. Harman for producing coins in contravention of the Coinage Act of 1850. This did not prevent coins from reaching numismatists, and today these coins are avidly sought after by collectors.

Investment in minor coins presents some questions to ponder: Will the collecting of minor coins by date and mintmark varieties ever be popular with collectors who reside within that particular country? Are the pieces relatively immune to the effects of restriking and counterfeiting (does the country have stringent laws against this?). Are the coins attractively designed and of pleasing appearance?

If the preceding questions can be answered in the affirmative, then chances are that a given coin will be a good investment—providing it is a scarce issue and is not high priced at the present time. Attractive profits have been made by many of our clients who have correctly anticipated that certain countries of the world—particularly such countries as Canada, Great Britain, France, Germany, Japan, Switzerland, and the Scandinavian countries—would develop numismatists

Interesting Minor (less than crown size) Coins of the World

Great Britain: Exceedingly rare coins of King Edward VIII; perhaps the only specimens in numismatic hands. Shown are the penny, shilling, farthing (¼ penny), sixpence, and half crown. The crown piece is shown on page 177.

German East Africa: 1890 1 rupie in silver.

Mexico: 1736 two-real or "two bit" piece in silver. Pillar design.

Hong Kong: Bronze cent of 1941. Very rare issue. Only a few were released.

German New Guinea: 1894 1 mark with the bird of paradise motif.

within their borders who would collect their own country's coinage by dates and mintmarks. The market for such specialized collecting is still in its infancy, and there are many attractive profits still to be made.

There is no single source where you can find complete information about coins of the world. Even a beginning library on the subject would fill a bookshelf. About $100 to $200 will buy you most of the popular reference books. In addition, such periodical publications as *Coin World* and *Numismatic News* and the specialized (coins of the world only; U.S. coins are not featured) *World Coin News*, to mention just three of several fine news sources printed in America, have offerings, information, and other news about coins of the world. Many fine catalogues are available from dealer members of the International Association of Professional Numismatists and other trade sources.

Coins of the world offer many attractive opportunities. Some study is required, and some intellectual curiosity will do no harm either! The standard of living is rising around the world, and with it is coming a growing interest in coin collecting. Buying coins today to satisfy the demand of tomorrow can be quite rewarding!

Postscript

Chapter 11
Postscript

It is my hope that the preceding pages have been of value to you. If you've read what I have had to say, you are now in a position to take advantage of the knowledge which has made untold millions of dollars for the customers of Bowers and Ruddy Galleries, Inc.

It is a great feeling to make money for others—it is like doing a favor for a fine friend. It is my sincere wish that this book will be your guide for making lots of money. Follow the precepts I have outlined, and the book should literally be worth its weight in gold to you.

Writing in the February-March 1959 issue of *Empire Topics,* I said: "Our outlook on the coin market for 1959? With the possible exception [of very modern issues] most United States coins should continue their steady appreciation in value. This will be particularly true of early material in choice condition . . ." In that issue of fifteen years ago James F. Ruddy and I offered for sale to our customers many different choice early coins. Without exception, each and every choice (Uncirculated or Proof) coin has *multiplied* in value.

1959 is not today, you might say—and this is true. However, the principles which guided successful coin investment in 1959 and have resulted in fortunes being made for our customers since then are still in effect today. A "treasure for the future" is awaiting you. Let this book be your passport!

Q. David Bowers

Some Facts
and
Figures

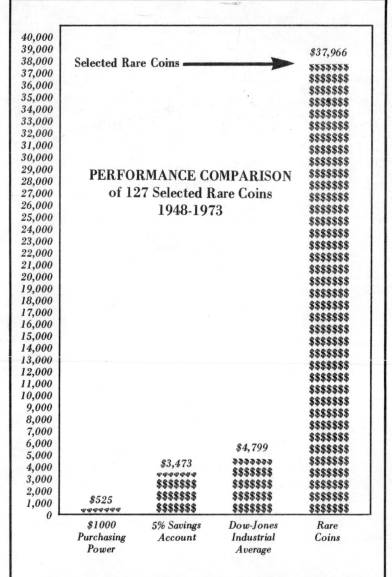

			$37,966

PERFORMANCE COMPARISON
of 127 Selected Rare Coins
1948-1973

Selected Rare Coins ⟶

40,000
39,000
38,000
37,000
36,000
35,000
34,000
33,000
32,000
31,000
30,000
29,000
28,000
27,000
26,000
25,000
24,000
23,000
22,000
21,000
20,000
19,000
18,000
17,000
16,000
15,000
14,000
13,000
12,000
11,000
10,000
9,000
8,000
7,000
6,000
5,000
4,000
3,000
2,000
1,000
0

$4,799

$3,473

$525

| $1000 Purchasing Power | 5% Savings Account | Dow-Jones Industrial Average | Rare Coins |

The above graph compares the price performance of the 127 selected classic coins described on page 193 and listed from page 193 through page 202. These classic coins are not necessarily representative of the coin market as a whole. Further, it is always important to remember that past performance is no guarantee or necessarily an indication of the future—for the future is always unknown.

Selected Coin Prices 1948-1974

1652 Pine Tree Shilling
Grade: Fine

Year	Price
1948	$40.00
1953	50.00
1958	70.00
1963	150.00
1968	300.00
1973	400.00
1977	500.00

Increase: 1150%

1786 Baby Hd. Vermont
Grade: Fine

Year	Price
1948	12.50
1953	15.00
1958	30.00
1963	65.00
1968	125.00
1973	325.00
1977	550.00

Increase: 4,300%

1855 Half Cent
Grade: Uncirculated

Year	Price
1948	5.00
1953	5.00
1958	11.00
1963	29.00
1968	65.00
1973	100.00
1977	280.00

Increase: 5,500%

1854 Cent
Grade: Uncirculated

Year	Price
1948	4.00
1953	4.00
1958	9.00
1963	20.00
1968	57.50
1973	100.00
1977	200.00

Increase: 4,900%

1859 Indian 1c
Grade: Uncirculated

Year	Price
1948	5.50
1953	7.50
1958	25.00
1963	65.00
1968	80.00
1973	175.00
1977	400.00

Increase 7,172%

1859 Indian 1c
Grade: Proof

Year	Price
1948	11.00
1953	12.50
1958	60.00
1963	275.00
1968	600.00
1973	650.00
1977	750.00

6,718%

Beginning on this page I give the price histories of selected United States coins, including regular copper, silver, and gold issues, plus colonials and commemoratives. I have included a number of major scarcities and rarities for two reasons: (1) These are numismatic classics of the past and will be the classics of the future, and (2) I have owned specimens of these coins in the past and have recommended them to clients over the years.

The prices given are from "A Guide Book of United States Coins" and are used with the permission of the Whitman Publishing Company. As the "cover date" of each issue is one year in advance of the publication date, my 1977 prices are from the 1978 edition (published in the summer of 1977), for example. For consistency I have used the catalogue figures; however, really choice examples of scarcities and rarities have very often sold for over "Guide Book" prices in the past. So, if anything, my 1977 figures are conservative for the better graded coins. Most pieces in this compilation will actually sell for more than the 1977 price listed.

In a number of instances I have given the price movement of the same coin in different grades: in Uncirculated grade and in Proof grade, for example. Taken as a whole, prices of choice rare coins have advanced steadily over the years. However, individual coin prices move upward at varying rates of advance. For this reason, I have always recommended diversification across many different choice and rare coin issues. You may consider this academic, however—for even the lesser performers sharply outpaced inflation!

The figures given from 1948 through 1973 represent five year intervals. To bring the prices up to date, the 1977 figures are added at the end—making this a 29-year study of rare coin prices.

Selected Coin Prices 1948-1974

1906 Indian 1c
Grade: Uncirculated
1948 ....0.75
1953 ....1.00
1958 ....3.25
1963 ....8.00
1968 ....9.25
1973 ....17.00
1977 ....34.00
Increase: 4,433%

1865 2c Piece
Grade: Uncirculated
1948 ....1.00
1953 ....2.00
1958 ....5.75
1963 ....12.00
1968 ....25.00
1973 ....57.00
1977 ......225.00
Increase: 22,400%

1865 Nickel 3c Piece
Grade: Uncirculated
1948 ....1.25
1953 ....1.75
1958 ....4.00
1963 ....8.50
1968 ....17.50
1973 ....32.50
1977 ......100.00
Increase: 7,900%

1882 Nickel 5c
Grade: Proof
1948 ....4.00
1953 ....6.00
1958 ....14.00
1963 ....30.00
1968 ....70.00
1973 ....80.00
1977 ......190.00
Increase: 4,650%

1910 Nickel 5c
Grade: Proof
1948 ....3.75
1953 ....5.50
1958 ....12.50
1963 ....23.50
1968 ....55.00
1973 ....60.00
1977 ......135.00
Increase: 3,500%

1913 TI Buffalo 5c
Grade: Uncirculated
1948 ....1.00
1953 ....1.00
1958 ....2.50
1963 ....5.50
1968 ....10.00
1973 ....16.00
1977 ....26.00
Increase: 2,500%

1852 Silver 3c Piece
Grade: Uncirculated
1948 ....3.50
1953 ....4.50
1958 ....8.50
1963 ....17.50
1968 ....45.00
1973 ....85.00
1977 ......195.00
Increase: 5,471%

1858 Silver 3c Piece
Grade: Uncirculated
1948 ....2.75
1953 ....5.00
1958 ....9.00
1963 ....30.00
1968 ....45.00
1973 ......275.00
1977 ......575.00
Increase: 20,809%

1859 Silver 3c Piece
Grade: Uncirculated
1948 ....3.00
1953 ....6.00
1958 ....12.00
1963 ....22.50
1968 ....50.00
1973 ....87.50
1977 ......210.00
Increase: 6,900%

1795 Half Dime
Grade: Uncirculated
1948 ....45.00
1953 ....55.00
1958 ......150.00
1963 ......500.00
1968 ......875.00
1973 ......1,200.00
1977 ......4,250.00
Increase: 9,344%

1797 15-Star Half Dime
Grade: Uncirculated
1948 ....80.00
1953 ......110.00
1958 ......175.00
1963 ......500.00
1968 ......1,150.00
1973 ......1,450.00
1977 ......5,500.00
Increase: 6,775%

1800 Half Dime
Grade: Fine
1948 ....15.00
1953 ....20.00
1958 ....45.00
1963 ......150.00
1968 ......285.00
1973 ......325.00
1977 ......360.00
Increase: 2,300%

1800 Half Dime
Grade: Uncirculated
1948 ....50.00
1953 ....75.00
1958 ......135.00
1963 ......450.00
1968 ......1,000.00
1973 ......1,250.00
1977 ......5,000.00
Increase: 9,900%

1832 Half Dime
Grade: Uncirculated
1948 ....2.50
1953 ....4.00
1958 ....8.00
1963 ....25.00
1968 ....70.00
1973 ......160.00
1977 ......425.00
Increase: 16,900%

Selected Coin Prices 1948-1974

1837 No-Stars 5c
Grade: Uncirculated
1948	7.50
1953	12.50
1958	45.00
1963	150.00
1968	260.00
1973	325.00
1977	825.00

Increase: 10,900%

1842 Half Dime
Grade: Uncirculated
1948	2.50
1953	4.00
1958	8.50
1963	17.50
1968	35.00
1973	85.00
1977	300.00

Increase: 11,900%

1853 Arrows 5c
Grade: Uncirculated
1948	1.50
1953	3.50
1958	7.50
1963	20.00
1968	50.00
1973	150.00
1977	400.00

Increase: 26,567%

1862 Half Dime
Grade: Uncirculated
1948	1.25
1953	2.50
1958	5.00
1963	12.50
1968	32.50
1973	85.00
1977	225.00

Increase: 17,900%

1862 Half Dime
Grade: Proof
1948	4.00
1953	8.50
1958	17.50
1963	45.00
1968	85.00
1973	100.00
1977	300.00

Increase: 7,400%

1796 Dime
Grade: Uncirculated
1948	125.00
1953	145.00
1958	300.00
1963	1,350.00
1968	2,150.00
1973	2,850.00
1977	7,000.00

Increase: 5,500%

1807 Dime
Grade: Uncirculated
1948	30.00
1953	40.00
1958	67.50
1963	230.00
1968	575.00
1973	900.00
1977	3,250.00

Increase: 10,733%

1827 Dime
Grade: Uncirculated
1948	8.50
1953	10.00
1958	17.50
1963	60.00
1968	150.00
1973	500.00
1977	2,000.00

Increase: 23,429%

1832 Dime
Grade: Uncirculated
1948	3.00
1953	4.00
1958	9.00
1963	25.00
1968	110.00
1973	400.00
1977	1,000.00

Increase: 33,233%

1837 No-Stars Dime
Grade: Uncirculated
1948	15.00
1953	22.50
1958	60.00
1963	175.00
1968	350.00
1973	675.00
1977	1,800.00

Increase: 11,900%

1853 Arrows Dime
Grade: Uncirculated
1948	2.50
1953	3.50
1958	6.50
1963	19.50
1968	50.00
1973	200.00
1977	450.00

Increase: 17,900%

1863 Dime
Grade: Uncirculated
1948	7.50
1953	8.50
1958	19.00
1963	33.50
1968	80.00
1973	175.00
1977	550.00

Increase: 7,233%

1863 Dime
Grade: Proof
1948	7.50
1953	11.00
1958	40.00
1963	57.50
1968	110.00
1973	185.00
1977	350.00

Increase 4,567%

Selected Coin Prices 1948-1974

1874 Dime
Grade: Fine
1948 ....1.00
1953 ....1.75
1958 ....9.00
1963 ....17.50
1968 ....19.00
1973 ....25.00
1977 ....27.50
Increase: 2,650%

1874 Dime
Grade: Uncirculated
1948 ....3.50
1953 ....9.00
1958 ....27.50
1963 ....70.00
1968 ......140.00
1973 ......250.00
1977 ......550.00
Increase: 15,614%

1874 Dime
Grade: Proof
1948 ....5.00
1953 ....10.00
1958 ....55.00
1963 ......125.00
1968 ......275.00
1973 ......350.00
1977 ......650.00
Increase: 12,900%

1901 Dime
Grade: Proof
1948 ....4.00
1953 ....6.00
1958 ....25.00
1963 ....40.00
1968 ....85.00
1973 ......120.00
1977 ......250.00
Increase: 6,150%

1942 Mercury Dime
Grade: Proof
1948 ....1.00
1953 ....1.00
1958 ....5.00
1963 ....7.50
1968 ....17.50
1973 ....22.00
1977 ....70.00
Increase: 6,900%

1875-S 20c Piece
Grade: Uncirculated
1948 ....6.00
1953 ....12.50
1958 ....25.00
1963 ....55.00
1968 ......145.00
1973 ......300.00
1977 ......850.00
Increase: 14,067%

1876 20c Piece
Grade: Proof
1948 ....20.00
1953 ....30.00
1958 ....57.50
1963 ......120.00
1968 ......265.00
1973 ......400.00
1977 ...1,300.00
Increase: 6,400%

1796 Quarter
Grade: Fine
1948 ....70.00
1953 ......100.00
1958 ......400.00
1963 ...1,700.00
1968 ...2,150.00
1973 ...2,250.00
1977 ...3,000.00
Increase: 4,186%

1796 Quarter
Grade: Uncirculated
1948 ......135.00
1953 ......250.00
1958 ......900.00
1963 ...2,750.00
1968 ...5,750.00
1973 ...8,000.00
1977 ...17,000.00
Increase: 12,493%

1806 Quarter
Grade: Fine
1948 ....6.50
1953 ....12.50
1958 ....27.50
1963 ....75.00
1968 ......110.00
1973 ......160.00
1977 ......210.00
Increase: 3,131%

1806 Quarter
Grade: Uncirculated
1948 ....30.00
1953 ....50.00
1958 ......135.00
1963 ......450.00
1968 ......750.00
1973 ...1,400.00
1977 ...4,400.00
Increase: 14,567%

1818 Quarter
Grade: Uncirculated
1948 ....15.00
1953 ....22.50
1958 ....60.00
1963 ......150.00
1968 ......400.00
1973 ...1,000.00
1977 ...2,600.00
Increase: 17,233%

1832 Quarter
Grade: Uncirculated
1948 ....5.00
1953 ....10.00
1958 ....17.50
1963 ....65.00
1968 ......200.00
1973 ......850.00
1977 ...1,500.00
Increase: 29,900%

Selected Coin Prices 1948-1974

1839 Quarter
Grade: Uncirculated
1948 .... 7.50
1953 .... 11.00
1958 .... 17.50
1963 .... 45.00
1968 .... 100.00
1973 .... 600.00
1977 ...... 1,600.00
Increase: 21,233%

1853 Arrows 25c
Grade: Uncirculated
1948 .... 4.50
1953 .... 7.50
1958 .... 20.00
1963 .... 40.00
1968 .... 200.00
1973 .... 600.00
1977 ...... 1,250.00
Increase: 27,677%

1861 Quarter
Grade: Uncirculated
1948 .... 2.25
1953 .... 3.50
1958 .... 6.00
1963 .... 17.50
1968 .... 37.50
1973 .... 165.00
1977 .... 450.00
Increase: 19,900%

1861 Quarter
Grade: Proof
1948 .... 9.00
1953 .... 10.00
1958 .... 30.00
1963 .... 60.00
1968 .... 125.00
1973 .... 215.00
1977 .... 600.00
Increase: 6,567%

1874 Quarter
Grade: Fine
1948 .... 1.25
1953 .... 6.00
1958 .... 14.00
1963 .... 25.00
1968 .... 28.00
1973 .... 35.00
1977 .... 30.00
Increase: 2,300%

1874 Quarter
Grade: Uncirculated
1948 .... 3.50
1953 .... 12.50
1958 .... 45.00
1963 .... 95.00
1968 .... 175.00
1973 .... 300.00
1977 .... 700.00
Increase: 19,900%

1874 Quarter
Grade: Proof
1948 .... 6.75
1953 .... 20.00
1958 .... 85.00
1963 .... 180.00
1968 .... 300.00
1973 .... 400.00
1977 .... 800.00
Increase: 11,752%

1878 Quarter
Grade: Uncirculated
1948 .... 2.25
1953 .... 3.00
1958 .... 5.50
1963 .... 13.50
1968 .... 37.50
1973 .... 165.00
1977 .... 350.00
Increase: 15,456%

1878 Quarter
Grade: Proof
1948 .... 4.50
1953 .... 6.50
1958 .... 24.00
1963 .... 42.50
1968 .... 70.00
1973 .... 185.00
1977 .... 450.00
Increase: 9,900%

1882 Quarter
Grade: Uncirculated
1948 .... 3.00
1953 .... 6.50
1958 .... 15.00
1963 .... 31.50
1968 .... 70.00
1973 .... 185.00
1977 .... 550.00
Increase: 18,233%

1882 Quarter
Grade: Proof
1948 .... 4.50
1953 .... 8.50
1958 .... 30.00
1963 .... 45.00
1968 .... 90.00
1973 .... 200.00
1977 .... 500.00
Increase: 11,011%

1908 Quarter
Grade: Uncirculated
1948 .... 3.50
1953 .... 5.00
1958 .... 8.00
1963 .... 15.00
1968 .... 37.50
1973 .... 115.00
1977 .... 235.00
Increase: 6,614%

1908 Quarter
Grade: Proof
1948 .... 5.50
1953 .... 9.00
1958 .... 45.00
1963 .... 62.50
1968 .... 110.00
1973 .... 180.00
1977 .... 410.00
Increase: 7,355%

Selected Coin Prices 1948-1974

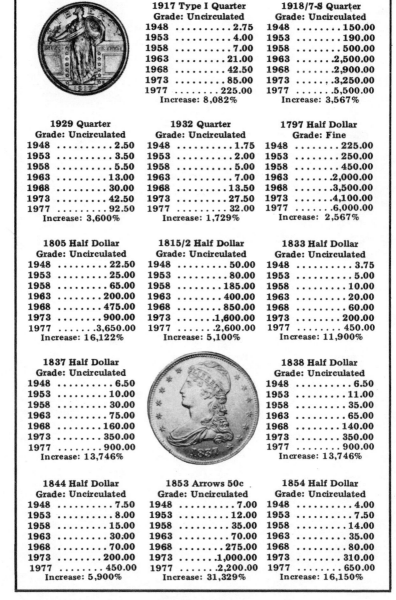

1917 Type I Quarter
Grade: Uncirculated
1948 .... 2.75
1953 .... 4.00
1958 .... 7.00
1963 .... 21.00
1968 .... 42.50
1973 .... 85.00
1977 .... 225.00
Increase: 8,082%

1918/7-S Quarter
Grade: Uncirculated
1948 .... 150.00
1953 .... 190.00
1958 .... 500.00
1963 ...... 2,500.00
1968 ...... 2,900.00
1973 ...... 3,250.00
1977 ...... 5,500.00
Increase: 3,567%

1929 Quarter
Grade: Uncirculated
1948 .... 2.50
1953 .... 3.50
1958 .... 5.50
1963 .... 13.00
1968 .... 30.00
1973 .... 42.50
1977 .... 92.50
Increase: 3,600%

1932 Quarter
Grade: Uncirculated
1948 .... 1.75
1953 .... 2.00
1958 .... 5.00
1963 .... 7.00
1968 .... 13.50
1973 .... 27.50
1977 .... 32.00
Increase: 1,729%

1797 Half Dollar
Grade: Fine
1948 .... 225.00
1953 .... 250.00
1958 .... 450.00
1963 ...... 2,000.00
1968 ...... 3,500.00
1973 ...... 4,100.00
1977 ...... 6,000.00
Increase: 2,567%

1805 Half Dollar
Grade: Uncirculated
1948 .... 22.50
1953 .... 25.00
1958 .... 65.00
1963 .... 200.00
1968 .... 475.00
1973 .... 900.00
1977 ...... 3,650.00
Increase: 16,122%

1815/2 Half Dollar
Grade: Uncirculated
1948 .... 50.00
1953 .... 80.00
1958 .... 185.00
1963 .... 400.00
1968 .... 850.00
1973 ...... 1,600.00
1977 ...... 2,600.00
Increase: 5,100%

1833 Half Dollar
Grade: Uncirculated
1948 .... 3.75
1953 .... 5.00
1958 .... 10.00
1963 .... 20.00
1968 .... 60.00
1973 .... 200.00
1977 .... 450.00
Increase: 11,900%

1837 Half Dollar
Grade: Uncirculated
1948 .... 6.50
1953 .... 10.00
1958 .... 30.00
1963 .... 75.00
1968 .... 160.00
1973 .... 350.00
1977 .... 900.00
Increase: 13,746%

1838 Half Dollar
Grade: Uncirculated
1948 .... 6.50
1953 .... 11.00
1958 .... 35.00
1963 .... 65.00
1968 .... 140.00
1973 .... 350.00
1977 .... 900.00
Increase: 13,746%

1844 Half Dollar
Grade: Uncirculated
1948 .... 7.50
1953 .... 8.00
1958 .... 15.00
1963 .... 30.00
1968 .... 70.00
1973 .... 200.00
1977 .... 450.00
Increase: 5,900%

1853 Arrows 50c
Grade: Uncirculated
1948 .... 7.00
1953 .... 12.00
1958 .... 35.00
1963 .... 70.00
1968 .... 275.00
1973 ...... 1,000.00
1977 ...... 2,200.00
Increase: 31,329%

1854 Half Dollar
Grade: Uncirculated
1948 .... 4.00
1953 .... 7.50
1958 .... 14.00
1963 .... 35.00
1968 .... 80.00
1973 .... 310.00
1977 .... 650.00
Increase: 16,150%

Selected Coin Prices 1948-1974

1863 Half Dollar
Grade: Uncirculated
1948 .... 4.50
1953 .... 5.00
1958 .... 10.00
1963 .... 24.00
1968 .... 65.00
1973 .... 200.00
1977 .... 600.00
Increase: 13,233%

1863 Half Dollar
Grade: Proof
1948 .... 11.00
1953 .... 15.00
1958 .... 55.00
1963 .... 90.00
1968 .... 165.00
1973 .... 260.00
1977 .... 650.00
Increase: 5,810%

1874 Half Dollar
Grade: Uncirculated
1948 .... 4.00
1953 .... 13.50
1958 .... 55.00
1963 .... 120.00
1968 .... 220.00
1973 .... 375.00
1977 .... 675.00
Increase: 16,775%

1874 Half Dollar
Grade: Proof
1948 .... 10.00
1953 .... 22.50
1958 .... 100.00
1963 .... 225.00
1968 .... 400.00
1973 .... 525.00
1977 .... 975.00
Increase: 5,650%

1876-CC Half Dollar
Grade: Uncirculated
1948 .... 6.00
1953 .... 6.50
1958 .... 15.00
1963 .... 35.00
1968 .... 65.00
1973 .... 190.00
1977 .... 650.00
Increase: 5,317%

1877 Half Dollar
Grade: Uncirculated
1948 .... 4.00
1953 .... 4.50
1958 .... 8.50
1963 .... 17.50
1968 .... 52.50
1973 .... 180.00
1977 .... 400.00
Increase: 9,900%

1877 Half Dollar
Grade: Proof
1948 .... 9.00
1953 .... 17.50
1958 .... 55.00
1963 .... 95.00
1968 .... 180.00
1973 .... 240.00
1977 .... 550.00
Increase: 6,011%

1886 Half Dollar
Grade: Uncirculated
1948 .... 6.00
1953 .... 11.00
1958 .... 37.50
1963 .... 85.00
1968 .... 115.00
1973 .... 260.00
1977 .... 650.00
Increase: 10,733%

1886 Half Dollar
Grade: Proof
1948 .... 12.50
1953 .... 35.00
1958 .... 95.00
1963 .... 105.00
1968 .... 160.00
1973 .... 275.00
1977 .... 575.00
Increase: 4,500%

1903 Half Dollar
Grade: Uncirculated
1948 .... 4.00
1953 .... 6.00
1958 .... 14.00
1963 .... 18.50
1968 .... 95.00
1973 .... 240.00
1977 .... 450.00
Increase: 11,150%

1903 Half Dollar
Grade: Proof
1948 .... 7.75
1953 .... 12.00
1958 .... 55.00
1963 .... 70.00
1968 .... 145.00
1973 .... 275.00
1977 .... 600.00
Increase: 7,642%

1916 Half Dollar
Grade: Uncirculated
1948 .... 5.00
1953 .... 12.00
1958 .... 21.00
1963 .... 30.00
1968 .... 100.00
1973 .... 130.00
1977 .... 275.00
Increase: 5,400%

1942 Half Dollar
Grade: Proof
1948 .... 2.50
1953 .... 3.50
1958 .... 11.00
1963 .... 23.00
1968 .... 50.00
1973 .... 65.00
1977 .... 125.00
Increase: 4,900%

1795 Silver Dollar
Grade: Fine
1948 .... 22.50
1953 .... 35.00
1958 .... 52.50
1963 .... 150.00
1968 .... 285.00
1973 .... 375.00
1977 .... 550.00
Increase: 2,344%

Selected Coin Prices 1948-1974

1795 Silver Dollar
Grade: Uncirculated
1948 ....135.00
1953 ....150.00
1958 ....300.00
1963 ....850.00
1968 ......1,300.00
1973 ......3,000.00
1977 .....15,000.00
Increase: 11,011%

1796 Silver Dollar
Grade: Uncirculated
1948 ....100.00
1953 ....125.00
1958 ....250.00
1963 ....550.00
1968 ......1,200.00
1973 ......2,500.00
1977 .....10,000.00
Increase: 9,900%

1847 Silver Dollar
Grade: Uncirculated
1948 ....12.50
1953 ....22.50
1958 ....36.00
1963 ....55.00
1968 ....135.00
1973 ....300.00
1977 ....900.00
Increase: 7,100%

1863 Silver Dollar
Grade: Uncirculated
1948 ....13.50
1953 ....22.00
1958 ....47.50
1963 ....75.00
1968 ....190.00
1973 ....350.00
1977 ....900.00
Increase: 6,567%

1863 Silver Dollar
Grade: Proof
1948 ....22.50
1953 ....35.00
1958 ....90.00
1963 ....130.00
1968 ....325.00
1973 ....450.00
1977 ......1,350.00
Increase: 5,900%

1870 Silver Dollar
Grade: Uncirculated
1948 ....10.00
1953 ....16.50
1958 ....22.50
1963 ....40.00
1968 ....95.00
1973 ....275.00
1977 ....725.00
Increase: 7,115%

1870 Silver Dollar
Grade: Proof
1948 ....16.00
1953 ....27.50
1958 ....50.00
1963 ....80.00
1968 ....275.00
1973 ....425.00
1977 ......1,350.00
Increase: 8,338%

1879 Silver Dollar
Grade: Proof
1948 ....10.00
1953 ....14.00
1958 ....55.00
1963 ....70.00
1968 ....210.00
1973 ....260.00
1977 ....600.00
Increase: 5,900%

1895 Silver Dollar
Grade: Proof
1948 ....80.00
1953 ....200.00
1958 ....650.00
1963 ......2,500.00
1968 ......4,750.00
1973 ......6,000.00
1977 ......8,250.00
Increase: 10,213%

1934-S Silver Dollar
Grade: Uncirculated
1948 ....12.50
1953 ....25.00
1958 ....40.00
1963 ....140.00
1968 ....225.00
1973 ....600.00
1977 ....950.00
Increase: 7,500%

1878-S Trade Dollar
Grade: Uncirculated
1948 ....5.00
1953 ....9.00
1958 ....16.50
1963 ....20.00
1968 ....80.00
1973 ....200.00
1977 ....475.00
Increase: 9,400%

1879 Trade Dollar
Grade: Proof
1948 ....15.00
1953 ....25.00
1958 ....55.00
1963 ....85.00
1968 ....350.00
1973 ....425.00
1977 ......1,400.00
Increase: 9,233%

1851 Gold Dollar
Grade: Uncirculated
1948 ....7.50
1953 ....10.00
1958 ....20.00
1963 ....45.00
1968 ....60.00
1973 ....175.00
1977 ....350.00
Increase: 4,567%

1855 Gold Dollar
Grade: Uncirculated
1948 ....12.50
1953 ....15.00
1958 ....37.50
1963 ....200.00
1968 ....400.00
1973 ......1,500.00
1977 ......2,100.00
Increase: 16,700%

Selected Coin Prices 1948-1974

1862 Gold Dollar
Grade: Uncirculated
1948 ....10.00
1953 ....10.00
1958 ....22.50
1963 ....57.50
1968 ....72.50
1973 ....175.00
1977 ....350.00
Increase: 3,400%

1875 Gold Dollar
Grade: Proof
1948 ....275.00
1953 ....275.00
1958 ....475.00
1963 ......2,000.00
1968 ......3,500.00
1973 ......4,000.00
1977 .....12,000.00
Increase: 4,264%

1796 NS $2½ Gold
Grade: Uncirculated
1948 ....275.00
1953 ....350.00
1958 ....950.00
1963 ......6,750.00
1968 ......7,750.00
1973 ......9,000.00
1977 .....25,000.00
Increase: 8,991%

1808 $2½ Gold
Grade: Uncirculated
1948 ....250.00
1953 ....300.00
1958 ....900.00
1963 ......6,000.00
1968 ......7,000.00
1973 ......7,500.00
1977 .....25,000.00
Increase: 9,900%

1831 $2½ Gold
Grade: Uncirculated
1948 ....75.00
1953 ....75.00
1958 ....115.00
1963 ....700.00
1968 ......1,000.00
1973 ......2,000.00
1977 ......6,500.00
Increase: 8,567%

1836 $2½ Gold
Grade: Uncirculated
1948 ....17.50
1953 ....17.50
1958 ....22.50
1963 ....100.00
1968 ....175.00
1973 ....300.00
1977 ......2,000.00
Increase: 11,329%

1848 CAL $2½ Gold
Grade: Uncirculated
1948 ....250.00
1953 ....275.00
1958 ....600.00
1963 ......5,000.00
1968 ......6,000.00
1973 ......7,250.00
1977 .....16,500.00
Increase: 6,500%

1908 $2½ Gold
Grade: Uncirculated
1948 ....9.00
1953 ....10.00
1958 ....16.00
1963 ....35.00
1968 ....42.50
1973 ....100.00
1977 ....200.00
Increase: 2,122%

1854 $3 Gold
Grade: Uncirculated
1948 ....27.50
1953 ....35.00
1958 ....77.50
1963 ....245.00
1968 ....350.00
1973 ....650.00
1977 ......1,750.00
Increase: 6,264%

1879 Flowing Hair $4
Grade: Proof
1948 ....500.00
1953 ....650.00
1958 ......1,450.00
1963 ......6,000.00
1968 ......8,000.00
1973 .....10,000.00
1977 .....20,000.00
Increase: 3,900%

1795 $5 Gold
Grade: Uncirculated
1948 ....150.00
1953 ....200.00
1958 ....400.00
1963 ......1,400.00
1968 ......2,400.00
1973 ......3,500.00
1977 .....10,000.00
Increase: 6,567%

1805 $5 Gold
Grade: Uncirculated
1948 ....50.00
1953 ....60.00
1958 ....100.00
1963 ....450.00
1968 ....750.00
1973 ....900.00
1977 ......2,900.00
Increase: 5,700%

1808 $5 Gold
Grade: Fine
1948 ....25.00
1953 ....40.00
1958 ....65.00
1963 ....200.00
1968 ....400.00
1973 ....425.00
1977 ....625.00
Increase: 2,400%

1808 $5 Gold
Grade: Uncirculated
1948 ....50.00
1953 ....60.00
1958 ....105.00
1963 ....425.00
1968 ....675.00
1973 ....750.00
1977 ......2,600.00
Increase: 5,100%

Selected Coin Prices 1948-1974

1835 $5 Gold
Grade: Uncirculated
1948 ....25.00
1953 ....25.00
1958 ....37.50
1963 ....110.00
1968 ....200.00
1973 ....500.00
1977 ......1,200.00
Increase: 4,700%

1908 $5 Gold
Grade: Uncirculated
1948 ....17.50
1953 ....17.50
1958 ....19.00
1963 ....32.50
1968 ....35.00
1973 ....100.00
1977 ....250.00
Increase: 1,329%

1795 $10 Gold
Grade: Uncirculated
1948 ....200.00
1953 ....250.00
1958 ....475.00
1963 ......1,500.00
1968 ......2,750.00
1973 ......4,500.00
1977 .....15,000.00
Increase: 7,400%

1799 $10 Gold
Grade: Fine
1948 ....60.00
1953 ....80.00
1958 ....140.00
1963 ....350.00
1968 ....550.00
1973 ....600.00
1977 ......1,150.00
Increase: 1,817%

1799 $10 Gold
Grade: Uncirculated
1948 ....90.00
1953 ....110.00
1958 ....215.00
1963 ....750.00
1968 ......1,200.00
1973 ......1,650.00
1977 ......5,500.00
Increase: 6,011%

1911 $10 Gold
Grade: Uncirculated
1948 ....37.50
1953 ....35.00
1958 ....37.50
1963 ....50.00
1968 ....75.00
1973 ....125.00
1977 ....285.00
Increase: 660%

1907 MCMVII $20
Grade: Uncirculated
1948 ....110.00
1953 ....150.00
1958 ....250.00
1963 ....850.00
1968 ....875.00
1973 ......2,000.00
1977 ......4,400.00
Increase: 3,900%

1928 $20 Gold
Grade: Uncirculated
1948 ....65.00
1953 ....65.00
1958 ....58.50
1963 ....80.00
1968 ....85.00
1973 ....175.00
1977 ....300.00
Increase: 361%

1893 Isabella 25c
Grade: Uncirculated
1948 ....10.00
1953 ....12.50
1958 ....36.00
1963 ....75.00
1968 ....75.00
1973 ....165.00
1977 ....275.00
Increase: 2,650%

1900 Lafayette $1
Grade: Uncirculated
1948 ....15.00
1953 ....22.50
1958 ....47.50
1963 ....100.00
1968 ....165.00
1973 ....450.00
1977 ....900.00
Increase: 5,900%

1915-S Pan-Pacific 50c
Grade: Uncirculated
1948 ....21.50
1953 ....25.00
1958 ....51.50
1963 ....80.00
1968 ....77.50
1973 ....265.00
1977 ....370.00
Increase: 1,621%

1928 Hawaiian 50c
Grade: Uncirculated
1948 ....32.50
1953 ....45.00
1958 ....150.00
1963 ....425.00
1968 ....450.00
1973 ......1,000.00
1977 ....950.00
Increase: 2,823%

1915-S Pan-Pacific $50
(Octagonal). Unc.
1948 ....475.00
1953 ....750.00
1958 ......1,850.00
1963 ......4,000.00
1968 ......4,900.00
1973 ......7,500.00
1977 .....13,000.00
Increase: 2,637%

Major Design Types of U.S. Coins

TYPES OF HALF CENTS
(1) 1793 Liberty cap type with head facing left.
(2) 1794-1797 Liberty cap with head facing right.
(3) 1800-1808 Draped bust type.
(4) 1809-1836 Classic head type.
(5) 1840-1857 Braided hair type.

TYPES OF LARGE CENTS
(1) 1793 Chain type.
(2) 1793 Wreath type.
(3) 1793-1796 Liberty cap type.
(4) 1796-1807 Draped bust type.
(5) 1808-1814 Classic head type.
(6) 1816-1839 Coronet type.
(7) 1839-1857 Braided hair type.

TYPES OF SMALL CENTS
(1) 1856-1858 Flying eagle type.
(2) 1859 Indian. Laurel wreath reverse.
(3) 1860-1864 Copper-nickel. Oak wreath reverse.
(4) 1864-1909 Indian. Bronze.
(5) 1909 V.D.B. Lincoln type.
(6) 1909-1958 Lincoln with wheat ears reverse.
(7) 1943 Steel cent.
(8) 1944-1945 Shell case metal cent.
(9) 1959 to date. Lincoln Memorial reverse type.

TWO-CENT PIECES
(1) 1864-1873 2c piece. One type issued.

NICKEL THREE-CENT PIECES
(1) 1865-1889 Nickel 3c piece. One type issued.

SILVER THREE-CENT PIECES
(1) 1851-1853 No outlines to star type.
(2) 1854-1858 Three outlines to star type.
(3) 1859-1873 Two outlines to star type.

NICKEL FIVE-CENT PIECES
(1) 1866-1867 Shield type with rays on reverse.
(2) 1867-1883 Shield type without rays.
(3) 1883 Liberty type without CENTS.
(4) 1883-1913 Liberty type with CENTS.
(5) 1913 Buffalo type with raised ground.
(6) 1913-1938 Buffalo type with level ground.
(7) 1938 to date. Jefferson type.
(8) 1942-1945 Jefferson "wartime" metal type.

Major Design Types of U.S. Coins

HALF DIMES
(1) 1794-1795 Flowing hair type.
(2) 1796-1797 Draped bust; small eagle type.
(3) 1800-1805 Draped bust; heraldic eagle type.
(4) 1829-1837 Capped bust type.
(5) 1837-1838 Liberty seated, no stars type.
(6) 1838-1860 Liberty seated, with stars type.
(7) 1853-1855 Arrows at date.
(8) 1860-1873 Liberty seated, legend on obverse.

DIMES
(1) 1796-1797 Draped bust; small eagle type.
(2) 1798-1807 Draped bust; heraldic eagle type.
(3) 1809-1828 Capped bust; large size type.
(4) 1828-1837 Capped bust; small size type.
(5) 1837-1838 Liberty seated, no stars type.
(6) 1838-1860 Liberty seated, with stars type.
(7) 1853-1855 Arrows at date.
(8) 1860-1891 Liberty seated, legend on obverse.
(9) 1873-1874 Arrows at date type.
(10) 1892-1916 Barber type.
(11) 1916-1945 Mercury type.
(12) 1946-1964 Roosevelt type. Silver metal.
(13) 1965 to date. Roosevelt type. Clad metal.

TWENTY-CENT PIECES
(1) 1875-1878 20c piece. One type issued.

QUARTER DOLLARS
(1) 1796 Draped bust; small eagle type.
(2) 1804-1807 Draped bust; heraldic eagle type.
(3) 1815-1828 Capped bust; large size type.
(4) 1831-1838 Capped bust; small size type.
(5) 1838-1865 Liberty seated, without motto type.
(6) 1853 Arrows at date; rays on reverse type.
(7) 1854-1855 Arrows at date type.
(8) 1866-1891 Liberty seated, with motto type.
(9) 1873-1874 Arrows at date type.
(10) 1892-1916 Barber type.
(11) 1916-1917 Liberty standing type I.
(12) 1917-1930 Liberty standing type II.
(13) 1932-1964 Washington. Silver metal.
(14) 1965 to date. Washington. Clad metal.
(15) 1776-1976 Bicentennial. Copper-nickel clad metal.
(16) 1776-1976 Bicentennial. Silver clad metal.

HALF DOLLARS
(1) 1794-1795 Flowing hair type.
(2) 1796-1797 Draped bust; small eagle type.
(3) 1801-1807 Draped bust; heraldic eagle type.
(4) 1807-1836 Capped bust; lettered edge type.
(5) 1836-1837 Capped bust; reeded edge; 50 CENTS reverse.

Major Design Types of U.S. Coins

(6) 1838-1839 Capped bust; reeded edge; HALF DOL. reverse.
(7) 1839-1866 Liberty seated, without motto type.
(8) 1853 Arrows at date; rays on reverse type.
(9) 1854-1855 Arrows at date type.
(10) 1866-1891 Liberty seated, with motto type.
(11) 1873-1874 Arrows at date type.
(12) 1892-1915 Barber type.
(13) 1916-1947 Liberty walking type.
(14) 1948-1963 Franklin type.
(15) 1964 Kennedy type. Silver metal.
(16) 1965 to date. Kennedy type. Clad metal.
(17) 1776-1976 Bicentennial. Copper-nickel clad metal.
(18) 1776-1976 Bicentennial. Silver clad metal.

SILVER DOLLARS
(1) 1794-1795 Flowing hair type.
(2) 1795-1798 Draped bust; small eagle type.
(3) 1798-1804 Draped bust; heraldic eagle type.
(4) 1836-1839 Gobrecht issues (patterns).
(5) 1840-1866 Liberty seated, no motto type.
(6) 1866-1873 Liberty seated, with motto type.
(7) 1878-1921 Morgan type.
(8) 1921-1935 Peace type.
(9) 1971 to date. Eisenhower type. Silver metal.
(10) 1971 to date. Eisenhower type. Clad metal.
(11) 1776-1976. Eisenhower bicentennial. Silver metal.
(12) 1776-1976. Eisenhower bicentennial. Clad metal.

TRADE DOLLARS
(1) 1873-1885 Trade dollar. One type issued.

GOLD DOLLARS
(1) 1849-1854 Liberty head type.
(2) 1854-1856 Indian head type; small head.
(3) 1856-1889 Indian head type; large head.

QUARTER EAGLES
(1) 1796 Capped bust, no stars type.
(2) 1796-1807 Capped bust right type; stars.
(3) 1808 Capped bust left type; large size.
(4) 1821-1834 Capped bust left type; smaller size.
(5) 1834-1839 Classic head type.
(6) 1840-1907 Coronet type.
(7) 1908-1929 Indian type.

THREE-DOLLAR GOLD PIECES
(1) 1854-1889 Three dollar gold piece. One type issued.

FOUR-DOLLAR GOLD PIECES
(1) 1879-1880 Flowing hair type. (Pattern).
(2) 1879-1880 Coiled hair type. (Pattern).

Major Design Types of U.S. Coins

HALF EAGLES ($5 GOLD)
(1) 1795-1798 Capped bust; small eagle type.
(2) 1795-1807 Capped bust right; heraldic eagle type.
(3) 1807-1812 Capped bust left type.
(4) 1813-1829 Capped head left; large size.
(5) 1829-1834 Capped head left; smaller size.
(6) 1834-1838 Classic head type.
(7) 1839-1866 Coronet type, without motto.
(8) 1866-1908 Coronet type, with motto.
(9) 1908-1929 Indian type.

EAGLES ($10 GOLD)
(1) 1795-1797 Capped bust right; small eagle type.
(2) 1797-1804 Capped bust right; heraldic eagle type.
(3) 1838-1866 Coronet type, without motto.
(4) 1866-1907 Coronet type, with motto.
(5) 1907-1908 Indian type, without motto.
(6) 1908-1933 Indian type, with motto.

DOUBLE EAGLES ($20 GOLD)
(1) 1849-1866 Liberty head type, without motto.
(2) 1866-1876 Liberty head type, with motto. TWENTY D. reverse.
(3) 1877-1907 Liberty head type, with motto. TWENTY DOLLARS
(4) 1907 MCMVII Saint-Gaudens Roman numerals issue.
(5) 1907-1908 Saint-Gaudens Arabic date; without motto.
(6) 1908-1933 Saint-Gaudens; with motto.

Index